# Little House in the Bush

# Little House in the Bush

Written and Illustrated by

## Wendy Hamilton

ZealAus Publishing

Little House in the Bush:
Growing Up in New Zealand


Copyright © 2020 by Wendy Hamilton
Illustrations © 2020 by Wendy Hamilton


www.zealauspublishing.com


All rights reserved. No part of this book may be reproduced or transmitted in any form or by any means without written permission of the author. Some names have been changed to protect the identity of persons.


ISBN: 978-1-925888-56-0 (e)
ISBN: 978-1-925888-57-7 (hc)
ISBN: 978-1-925888-58-4 (sc)

# Dedication

For Rachel

# Contents

| | |
|---|---|
| The Land Hunt | 1 |
| Trolls, Vikings, and the Scotch | 15 |
| Less Land Than We Thought | 22 |
| Walking the boundary line | 30 |
| Cattle | 43 |
| Short on Grass | 52 |
| The Cattle Hunt | 57 |
| A Bigger Little House in the Bush | 64 |
| Antoinette's Bedroom | 71 |
| Antoinette's Lipstick | 80 |
| Substitute Horses | 95 |
| A Beaut Bargain | 102 |
| On the Brink of Horse Ownership | 110 |
| Not a Book Horse | 116 |
| A Bargain is Not Always a Bargain | 124 |
| Larry Lamb | 130 |
| Problems with Larry | 139 |
| Goodbye to Town Life | 146 |
| About the Author | 153 |
| Other Children's Books By Wendy Hamilton | 154 |

**Little House in the Bush**

# The Land Hunt.

"Town living is making the girls soft," said Dad looking at me and my two sisters as we lounged about reading.

"What do you mean?" asked Mum, her eyebrows shooting up and her knitting needles slowing. "You're not thinking of shifting us to some remote place in the bush are you?" The needles stopped completely at this appalling idea, "I love town life."

"Not permanently," said Dad, "I just thought if we sold the beach section and Three Bear's Cottage, we could buy a block of land."

"SELL and BUY," Mum echoed, dropping her knitting in excitement, her eyes glazed over like a kid looking through a sweetshop window. Mum loved the cut and thrust of wheeling and dealing. Her father had been a salesman and her childhood homes were perched above dairies or shoe shops.

# Wendy Hamilton

"Wendy is thirteen, it is high time our children experienced their pioneering heritage," continued Dad, imagining bush hikes and possum hunting.

"Three Bears is not returning much rent," said Mum, thinking of their little old miner's cottage, "but we could sell it for a good profit."

"A bit of bush would be nice, my great grandfather cleared ten acres of timber by hand," said Dad, swinging an imaginary axe.

"Fifty-acre blocks are cheap in the Hokianga currently," said Mum, tapping her tooth with the end of an empty knitting needle, "now is a good time to buy land in the Far North, in ten years' time it will be worth a fortune."

"I want to be able to drop the girls off in the bush by helicopter and have them survive off the land for a month," said Dad, sharpening an imaginary bush knife.

"Are we going for a helicopter ride?" asked Antoinette, looking up from her book suddenly. Her top lip elongated into haughtiness and her normal voice changed into a British accent, "that would be something to tell the girls at school," she said, adjusting the plastic tiara on her head.

"No, no," said Dad hastily, "you're not really going up in a helicopter, it is just an expression."

"Oh, I might have known," said Antoinette, dropping back into her normal accent, "I hate living in this family, I'm twelve and I've never done anything glamourous. Meagan's father has a sports car and Tony's mother lets

## Little House in the Bush

her wear lipstick, but I never get to do anything!"

"We should get a lot more for the beach section than we paid for it," said Mum ignoring Antoinette's outburst, "since the Council drained the swamp the price of land has gone up."

"A bit of pasture would be nice," said Dad, "I used to milk the family cow when I was three."

"Cows," said Mum losing the glazed look, "I don't like the sound of milking a cow."

"No, no," said Dad reassuringly, "we couldn't milk a cow because we won't be living there, I thought I could run a few steers on the land to make a bit of extra cash."

"Extra cash is always a good idea," said Mum glazing over again. "I'll call all the Real Estate agents tomorrow."

"Good," said Dad, visualizing himself planting a field of corn.

Mum got to work and before long Three Bears and the beach section were sold. That was the selling over and done with. Now for the really fun bit, tracking down a bargain. "Got any fifty-acre snips in Northland?" Mum asked the first Real Estate agent on her list.

"Snips? I don't quite understand."

"Bargains, I'm looking for cheap land," said Mum, naming a price. "Not for that sort of money, Lady," said Agent One rudely, "this is 1975 not 1920."

Agent Two, Three, and Four, responded in the same way, only a little more politely.

# Wendy Hamilton

*"Town living is making the girls soft"*

## Little House in the Bush

"I have one you might like," said Agent Five, "when would you like me to take you to see it?"

"Tomorrow when the kids are at school," said Mum.

The day was a wild success; the weather was beautiful, the car was new, and there were no children tagging along.

"I've found paradise," raved Mum, "the view is spectacular, it looks all the way down the Hokianga harbour."

"How many acres?" asked Dad.

"Fifty," said Mum, "all with fabulous views."

"Was it bush or pasture?"

"Steep pasture with a bit of bush, but the view, oh Doggal," said Mum (using his pet name) "I wish you had been there, spectacular!"

"We could go and have a look at it on Saturday," said Dad.

"Yes," said Mum, "that's a marvellous idea."

Saturday dawned bright and beautiful, that, however, was one of the few things the two trips had in common. The Agent's car was sleek like a wasp, the engine purred, and the black vinyl seats smelled new. Where as our car bulged like a bumblebee, the engine rattled, and red leather seats were crazed with age. Moreover, they tasted salty, and herein lay the chief difference between the two days; no children lolled in the backseat of the agent's car, chewing the upholstery and grumbling.

"Are we nearly there yet?" Rubella whined as the car bounced and juddered along the gravel road.

## Wendy Hamilton

"No, we have a wee way to go," said Mum brightly, "see who can spot the most white horses."

"There's one," I said, pointing out the window smugly.

"There is another one," said Rubella.

"That one doesn't count," I said, "it has black spots."

"It does so count!"

"Does not."

"Does so," Rubella's voice was rising.

"Does not," I shouted.

"Quieten down, you two," said Mum, swivelling around and fixing us with a hard look.

"Ooh look, there's a castle," gasped Antoinette pointing at the ruins of an old meat works.

That kept us happy for a few minutes, and the three humped bridges that left our tummies behind, amused us for a few more.

"Are we nearly there yet?" asked Rubella.

"We still have a bit to go," said Mum, "but the view when we get there makes the whole trip worthwhile."

"I bet it won't," I mumbled, leaning forward and chewing on the back of Mum's seat.

"It's spectacular," raved Mum, "in fact, I will pay anyone fifty cents who can look at that panoramic view and not agree that it is paradise."

Antoinette, Rubella, and I, stared at each other in wonder. In the seventies, fifty cents was a fortune. For the next hour we sat quietly, thinking of all the ways we could spend it. I still had not decided between an ice

## Little House in the Bush

cream or a bottle of fizz when we arrived.

"Here we are, said Mum, as Dad stopped the car next to a For-Sale sign.

We tumbled out in a dishevelled heap and climbed over a sagging wire fence.

"It's this side of the hill," said Mum, pointing out the boundaries. "Come and see the view."

The hill was steep and we puffed as we trudged behind her, eager to earn our prize. At the top we paused to get our breath.

"Now what do you think of that?" asked Mum dramatically, pointing to the stunning view of glittering water and bush-clad hills, "is that not Paradise?"

"Nah," I said, deciding fizz would be better than an ice cream.

"Nah," said Rubella, trying to work out how many gobstoppers fifty cents would buy.

"Boring," said Antoinette, thinking of a big bag of bubblegum.

Mum slumped into the long grass in a black mood, while we kids skipped about exploring. On the other side of Paradise was another block of land, it too was for sale. Unlike Paradise, it was covered with brambles and had no view. It did, however, sport a pear tree laden with fruit; moreover, they were ripe. We gorged ourselves until we were sticky with juice.

"Mum and Dad should buy this land," I said filling my sunhat with fruit, "then we could eat pears every time we came here."

## Wendy Hamilton

"Yeah, let's tell them," said Antoinette climbing back over the fence that separated the two properties.

Oddly, Mum was not impressed with our suggestion. "We are going home," she said, stomping down the hill.

"The trip was a nightmare," moaned Mum to Agent Five on Monday morning. "Not only did the little hounds shatter my dream, they had the gall to insist I pay up when we came to the first dairy. I think we need something closer to home. Do you have any snips within a twenty-mile radius?"

"I have three that might suit you," said Agent Five, "when would you like me to take you to look at them?"

The thought of a childless day cruising around properties was tempting. Mum, however, was not going to fall into the trap of unreality twice.

"Just give me a list of properties and directions," she said, sighing regretfully, "I'll go in my own car on the weekend."

So Saturday morning we set out for Maungatapere a mere thirty minutes away.

The first property was the best value for money. The entire fifty acres lay in a sloping jungle of tall grass unbroken by trees or anything interesting. Antoinette, Rubella, and I, loathed it on sight. We stood on the verge of the road scowling.

"It has a view," said Mum, looking at the bland expanse of fields beyond, "not spectacular like the view at Paradise of course, but at least it is some sort of view."

"Good clean land, you could run a lot of cattle on

## Little House in the Bush

this," said Dad, climbing the fence and pushing his way through the waist-high vegetation. "Come on kids, I think there is a stream at the bottom."

"The grass is too long," whined Rubella.

"Don't whine," said Dad, "nine is too old to whine like a baby, get a bit of backbone. Come on girls climb the fence."

"I don't want too, I hate it here," I said, crossing my arms and digging in my heels.

"I wish you had let me go to Meagan's place for the weekend," said Antoinette, flopping onto the ground pouting, "her father was going to take us to the pictures in his sports car."

"Well, you can all stay there while Mum and I go," said Dad disappointed.

"What a pity I didn't think to bring gumboots," said Mum with false regret. "There is another block of land for sale down the road," she added hastily. "Perhaps we should go and have a look at that instead."

"Oh, all right," said Dad, retracing his steps through the wake of flattened grass.

The second property was charming. It was dotted with trees, and undulated picturesquely; a winding creek meandered through its dips and folds.

"I like this one," said Antoinette.

"It is a pretty little Dingle Dell," admitted Mum, "but it's not such good value as Long Grass."

"It's got lots of beautiful daisies," said Rubella, gathering bunches of bright yellow flowers.

## Wendy Hamilton

"Ragwort," said Dad gloomily, "kill a horse in no time.".

"And blackberries," I enthused, stuffing my mouth with the juicy berries.

"Yes, blackberries and gorse," said Dad even more gloomily, "getting rid of them is hard work."

"Let's look at Mount Tiger," said Mum, glancing at the last property on her list.

"Mount Tiger, cool," I said, fascinated by the name.

"Can we see the tiger?" said Rubella, as we trudged back to the road.

"There won't really be a tiger," said Dad. "There are no tigers in New Zealand."

"I saw a tiger once, when Meagan's father took her and me to the circus," said Antoinette in a British accent.

"Perhaps it escaped from the circus," said Rubella. "If we find it, we might get a reward."

"There is no tiger," said Mum firmly, as she opened the front door of the car.

"When we find it, I'm going to buy a yellow leather dress with the reward money," said Antoinette, climbing in the back, "and I will wear it when the newspaper reporters take my picture. That will be something to show the girls at school."

"There is no Tiger," said Dad, sliding in behind the steering wheel.

"That's right," (as the eldest, I thought I knew more than the other two) "it's called Mount Tiger because the mountain looks like a tiger."

## Little House in the Bush

"It's not really a mountain," said Dad, "there are no actual mountains in Northland. Mount Tiger is a range of steep hills."

"It could have escaped from the zoo," said Rubella, doubling the possibility of a tiger.

"There are lots of places on a mountain for a tiger to hide," said Antoinette, thinking of her new dress.

"That's right," said Rubella, slamming the door shut.

·····

The drive to the Mount Tiger Property was an experience. The car growled as we ground along in second gear over the red gravel road that rose and plunged along the ridge.

"Wow, this is like riding the rollercoaster Meagan's father took us on," said Antoinette, forgetting to be British in her excitement.

"I'd rather ride a rollercoaster," I said, peering out the window at the steep drop on either side of the road, "it's safer."

"Does anyone need a car sickness pill?" asked Mum weakly, as the car slewed around a hairpin bend and bounced in and out of potholes.

"Nobody needs one," said Dad, as we shuddered to a halt beside a For-Sale sign, "we are here."

"This looks pleasant," said Mum, climbing out of the car stiffly, "that is a very nice paddock," she added, looking at the field of lush grass.

"Yes," said Dad looking pleased, "I was expecting steep land, but this is gently rolling."

## Wendy Hamilton

"I don't see any tiger," said Rubella disappointed.

"You are such a baby," said Antoinette, "it won't wander around in the open, it will be hiding."

"Yes, there are many places to hide on a mountain, it might be in the bush over there," I said, pointing at the bush bordering the field.

"A thousand-acre bush reserve, now that's the best neighbor to have," said Dad, drawing our attention to a Department of Conservation sign nearby.

"A thousand acres!" squeaked Rubella delighted, "a tiger could easily hide in a thousand acres."

"This isn't a mountain, and there is no tiger," said Dad patiently.

"Your father is right, there is no tiger," quavered Mum as she looked at the thick dark bush nervously, "there is no tiger," she repeated in a tone lacking conviction.

"Obviously the reserve is the left boundary," said Dad changing the subject, "but how far along the road is the right boundary?"

"A quarter of a mile," said Mum, examining her list.

Dad squinted into the distance, "it must include those two paddocks," he said, pointing at the neighbouring fields.

He pushed the gate open and we trooped into the field. At forty acres it was the smallest of the three blocks and (at first glance) the flattest. We were in for a surprise when we got deeper in, however. A gale whooshed up around us as we breasted a slight rise

# Little House in the Bush

and the land plunged into a deep bush-clad valley that snaked into a glimpse of the harbour.

"What view!" enthused Dad, "land like that will be crawling with possums and wild pigs! Just the thing to bring out the pioneering spirit in the girls."

"Spectacular in a wild way," agreed Mum in a faint voice that the wind whipped away.

"There could be a hundred tigers living down there," shouted Rubella.

"The girls at school will be so jealous of my yellow dress," beamed Antoinette.

And I, leaning on the wind with my arms outstretched, felt my soul soar with the hawks riding the thermal waves.

It was unanimous, we had found heaven on earth.

"You won't regret it," said Agent Five, handing Mum and Dad the title deeds on Monday morning. "If you decide to subdivide and sell the small paddock on the other side of the road, keep me in mind."

"There is a paddock across the road?" said Mum, delighted by this windfall.

"Yes, didn't you realize?"

"No."

"It's over here," said Agent Five, drawing a diagram on the back of an old envelope.

"Perhaps I should have gone with you after all," joked Mum, "we might have bought the wrong land."

"No harm done," laughed Agent Five, "nobody complains when they get more land than they expected."

"Especially when it is flat pasture," said Dad, "it is impossible to work out where the boundaries are in the bush."

"Provided you don't intend to clear it," said Agent Five, "it doesn't really matter, because you can go anywhere you like in the Reserve, and after that, it's all forestry."

"I might clear a couple of acres," said Dad, thinking of his grandfather's monstrous handsaw, "but only because I want to teach the girls how to fell a tree, I love the bush."

"You'll be alright then," said Agent Five, shaking his hand in farewell.

**Little House in the Bush**

# Trolls, Vikings, and the Scotch

Mount Tiger was a mere twenty-minute drive from our house in town. It felt as remote and wild, however, as the back of the boondocks. Because the bush is inhospitable without some sort of dwelling (especially when it is wet) Dad got stuck into providing shelter. On Saturday morning we gathered in the backyard as he dismantled a shed. The small shed was a leftover from his building days and designed to be portable. It was square with a flat roof and corrugated iron walls, a door and a window. Antoinette, Rubella, and I used it as a playhouse. Next to it stood a tall thin outhouse (another remnant of Dad's building days.) We did not play in this shed, however, because it housed a bucket topped with a toilet seat. The wildness of Mount Tiger had stirred up Dad's pioneering spirit, and his tools were not helping matters. The sawhorse he stood on, and many of the hand-tools in his toolbox, had once belonged to his grandfather.

"Your great-great-grandfather bought this wrecking bar all the way from the Shetland Isles to New Zealand in a sailing ship," said Dad, inserting it carefully between the shed's roof and walls.

"Where is the Shetland Isles?" said Rubella, tickling the cat's tummy.

"It is way past England, almost as far North as you can go," said Dad, levering the bar up and down, "he and his family sailed from the top of the world all the way down to the bottom of the world. You kids have both ends of the earth in your heritage."

He stopped levering and expertly removed a few strategic nails.

"Are there castles in the Shetland Isles?" asked Antoinette, twirling about on one foot (she was hoping for something blue in her blood.)

Dad coughed awkwardly because he did not want to admit he didn't know. He got around it by saying mysteriously, "you will know when you are older."

Antoinette was thrilled. Dad's reticence confirmed her suspicions. It was true, she really was a princess.

"I'm going to lift off the roof and slide it down for you to catch," said Dad hoisting up one end. "Spread around, don't all go to one spot. Rubella, help Mum, Wendy and Antoinette go over the other side."

We caught it and shuffled awkwardly with it past the

## Little House in the Bush

[1]chooks-house. Dad leaping off the saw-horse, helped us position it on the trailer.

"The Johnson men were so short and fierce the villagers thought they were trolls," said Dad carrying on with his story as we walked back to the shed, "they used to rush out and raid the villages."

"And castles?" asked Antoinette.

"Possibly," conceded Dad, detaching the front wall from the sides and floor, "descended from Vikings we are. Take a corner each, one, two, three, lift."

"I always knew I was kidnapped at birth," puffed Antoinette, staggering under the weight of her end, "the rest of you are such peasants."

We ignored her; it was not the first time we had suffered her scorn.

"Lie it down carefully," said Dad, sliding the wall on top of the roof like a stack of pancakes, "I don't want the window broken."

We did as we were told.

"Harold do we need to hold on to the other walls to stop them from falling," asked Mum, as we wandered back.

"Not yet, but the next wall you will," said Dad. A tough nail screeched as he wrenched it out. "Your ancestors cleared huge kauri trees off the land and built a track over treacherous mountains," said Dad, returning to his subject as he pulled out several more nails. "Now we have a chance to follow in their footsteps."

---
1    chicken coop

## Wendy Hamilton

"I was hoping to spend my weekends reading," said Mum, looking alarmed.

I felt sorry for Dad. His pep talk on pioneering was not going well. "Do we really come from Vikings?" I asked kindly.

"Yes," said Dad, beaming at my interest.

I could not imagine Dad as a Viking or a troll. He looked far more like an industrious garden gnome as he finished pulling the shed apart. Not a fishing gnome (Dad was no good at fishing) he was a Patting-Sitting-Deer gnome. And instead of a blue coat and a red pointy hat, Dad wore work boots, a brown jersey, and a homespun [2]beanie hat.

Mum also was gnome sized. Unlike Dad (who was stocky like a Shetland pony) Mum was fine-boned with tiny hands and feet. Her mother was Scottish. Nana had immigrated to New Zealand with her family when she was eighteen. Like the Scottish stereotype, Nana was canny with money, a trait Mum inherited. In addition to seeing land as a good investment, Mum saw Mount Tiger as free holidays.

"What about the toilet, Harold?" she said, as we dumped the last wall on the trailer, "do we have to make a second trip?" Her brow furrowed as she thought of the cost of gas.

"No, it can sit on top."

Relief, smoothed Mum's brow.

"Rubella, put the bucket and toilet seat in the back

---

2     Knitted hat

## Little House in the Bush

of the car," said Dad, walking over to the outhouse and opening the rickety door, "the rest of you catch the shed when I tip it over."

"Ooh, why do I have to carry the toilet," fussed Rubella.

"Because you are the smallest and weakest," said Antoinette, pleased she didn't have the job.

"Stop your fussing," said Dad handing it to her, "it's clean."

Rubella took them gingerly. She held them with two fingers, one in each hand, as far away from her body as possible. Dad sighed as he watched her mince towards the car, shaping his family into tough pioneers was going to take longer than he thought.

"OK, everyone," he said pushing the outhouse over, "take a corner each and lift on the count of three. One, two, three."

We hoisted it up and staggered over to the trailer.

"Now put it on top of the load," puffed Dad. We heaved it up and Dad slid it into the middle.

"Do you need us anymore, Harold?" asked Mum.

"No," said Dad, throwing a rope over the load.

"Does anyone need to use the bathroom before we go?" asked Mum, heading for the house.

There was a sudden stampede as we all rushed inside. None of us were keen on the bucket toilet, and the longer we could delay using it, the better.

When we got back, Dad had finished securing the load.

## Wendy Hamilton

"Everyone, get in the car," he said, tying a white rag on the overhanging outhouse.

The car was a 1960s Hillman Hunter station wagon. As befitting a family of gnomes, it was a lightweight car with a small engine. Dad's Viking blood was only evident in the trailer; a massive wooden thing, twice the length of the car. It was a lot to ask the little car to pull (without adding a shed and an outhouse on top.)

"Do you think we'll make it up Horror hill?" asked Mum anxiously, referring to a steep snaking part of the road.

"It will be fine," said Dad, sliding in behind the steering wheel and slamming the door shut. He put the car in first, and it moved sluggishly up our long driveway and into the traffic.

The trip within the city limits was event-free, and even the first set of hills we scaled without trouble.

"Climb over the seat into the back, kids," said Dad, as we approached the dreaded hill. He clutched the steering wheel and leaned forward like a Viking captain at the helm of his ship. "Remember to keep your weight over the wheels!" he commanded in the tone of Ivan the Terrible, "I'll try to gain us some momentum."

He pushed the accelerator to the floor as he spoke. Then with wheels spinning and the motor screaming, we zoomed down a slope and roared up the cliff face of Horror Hill. The trailer followed, waggling like a duck's bottom. Three-quarters of the way up, on the sharp bend, the car slowed to a stop before sliding backwards.

## Little House in the Bush

"Everyone out and get behind the trailer," yelled Dad, wrenching on the handbrake. "Anne you drive," he yelled, leaping out and chocking big rocks behind the back wheels of the car.

We tumbled out of the car in a panic, as Mum slid over to the driver's side.

"OK Anne, put it in first and give it the gun," Dad shouted, "push kids, push."

Mum put her foot to the floor and the car, engine shrieking, wheels spinning, and flicking up red gravel, crawled forward. Inch by inch, muscles straining and eyes popping, we pushed our burden up the last part of the hill. Over the crest, the road flattened and the car pulled away from us, moving a little way on its own before stopping. It idled like a panting dog and smelled of hot oil, as Mum slid back to her seat and the rest of us clambered in.

"Boy, I'm glad we didn't have to unload the trailer and carry everything up," said Dad, as we continued our journey.

A groan of relief went through the car over the horrible possibility. From then on, our emotions followed the road. They sank as we crawled up steep inclines and rose as we sailed down the other side. Fortunately, however, the rest of the trip was uneventful. It was not until we had everything unloaded and two walls assembled that disaster struck.

**Wendy Hamilton**

# Less Land Than We Thought

A powerful Mercedes car roared through the gate, rolled across the grass, and jerked to a halt. A tall man with an irate face leapt out

"What do you think you are doing?" he yelled, striding over in long-legged bounces.

"Putting up a shed," said Dad mildly, "we bought this land last week."

"Oh no you didn't," said the man with conviction. "This is my land, the boundary is over there." He pointed to a distant fence. "Here I'll show you the boundary lines," he said, slapping a map on the hood of his car and rolling it out.

Antoinette, Rubella and I made daisy chains and lolled about on the shed floor while Mum and Dad

## Little House in the Bush

sorted out the problem. At length the Mercedes drove away. "What happened?" I asked, throwing my daisy chain down.

"I should have gone with the Agent," said Mum bitterly, as we loaded everything back on the trailer.

"We measured the road frontage from the Reserve boundary, instead of the end of the little paddock across the road," said Dad.

"Fancy getting that puny little slither of dirt instead of this lovely big field," said Mum, even more bitterly. "Do we still even want this land? We might be able to get out of the deal because it's a third less than we expected."

"Only a third less pasture," said Dad, as we climbed back into the car and drove out the gate. "We have a third more bush than we realized."

"Yes," said Mum, shuddering at the thought. "But it is so steep and such a wilderness. We don't even know where the boundaries are."

"We will find them," said Dad, his eyes gleaming at the thought. "I saw the tops of Kauri trees down there." He drove a short distance down the road.

"At least we still have the piece with the view," said Mum softening, "that's worth a lot."

"That's right, and don't forget the spring. It's a big thing to have a water source," said Dad, stopping the car outside the gate, "what do you kids think, do you still like it here?"

"Yes," we chorused.

# Wendy Hamilton

*By noon the shed was assembled*

## Little House in the Bush

"Then we are all agreed," said Dad, driving through the gate.

"At least this bit has a gravel driveway," said Mum sighing, "that's a saving."

"What about putting the shed here?" said Dad, stopping under a stand of lovely big Totara trees.

"Oh yes," said Mum smiling.

We tumbled out and rushed about exploring, while Dad loosened the rope on the trailer. When he had finished, he coiled it up and threw it in the back of the car.

"Come and help girls," he called, sliding the outhouse off the top of the pile.

This time nobody stopped us, and by noon the shed was assembled. Moreover, we had a crude but functional toilet.

"Twelve o'clock, time for lunch," said Dad, who had rigid habits when it came to mealtimes. "You get the food while I set up the table," he said to Mum.

Mum nodded, and opened the back door of the car, while Dad flicked the tailboard of the trailer down and pulled out an old door and two sawhorses.

"Wendy and Antoinette, bring a sawhorse and Rubella, get the campstools out of the trailer," he said hoisting the door onto its side and carrying it towards the shed.

It was a small job to lie the door on the sawhorses and set the stools around it. Mum arrived just as we finished, and put a basket, a bottle of milk, and a thermos flask on the table.

"Did you bring the orange drink?" I asked hopefully.

"Yes," said Mum, pulling a packet of orange-flavoured powder out of the basket and handing it to me, along with a cup. "Dad is bringing the water."

"Here you are," said Dad, dumping a four-gallon drum on the end of the table.

Mum plunked a breadboard on the table and cut a loaf into thick slabs before spreading them with butter and [3]marmite. We munched away happily, taking in our new surroundings. When we were finished, Mum screwed the top back on the thermos flask.

"You set up the bunks, Harold, while I take the girls to get water for the dishes," said Mum, handing us buckets.

"Right oh," said Dad, brushing crumbs off the table with his hands.

We skipped after Mum to a small fenced area nearby. The land inside the fence was broken into tiny lumpy islands. Between each island, water seeped into small pools until they overflowed in a continuous trickle that ran down the hill and into the steep valley below. I put my barefoot on the middle wire of the fence and sprang up. The wire squeaked and bit into the arch of my foot as I swung my leg over the fence, and the bucket banged against my calve as I jumped down. I scooped up a load of water and staggered back to the fence. "Boy this is

---

3    Iconic New Zealand food spread made from yeast extract

## Little House in the Bush

heavy," I said.

"Tip a bit out," said Mum who was also having trouble. "Antoinette, get over the fence and the rest of us will pass the buckets to you."

"I wish I was at Meagan's place," said Antoinette in a British accent, as she dumped her bucket down and squeezed through the wires. "She doesn't have to carry water like a peasant. She has a fridge full of soft drinks and she can have one whenever she likes."

"Here, take this," I said sourly, passing her the buckets one by one.

"How are you getting on, Doggal?" asked Mum, when we got back.

"Nearly there," said Dad, carrying a bed frame into the shed. We heard banging as he manoeuvred about in the tight space, slotting it between the walls like a shelf. There was just enough room for a set of bunks on either side of the door; three on one side and two on the other. Dad had made the bunks himself the way his pioneering great grandfather had. Each bed base had a wooden perimeter and a hollow interior which Dad stretched rope across in a taut grid. The bunks were like our mixed ancestry; they were small enough for trolls and hard enough for Vikings. Moreover, the rope was free, because we found it washed up on the beach after a wild storm, which kept the Scotch happy.

"Here you go, Mother," said Dad chivalrously, throwing a mattress on the only bed with enough headroom for sitting up.

## Wendy Hamilton

"This is really starting to feel like home," said Mum, popping a sleeping bag and pillow on top. "Now all we need is a kitchen," she added, looking at the small space between the bunks.

"You get the camp stove and I'll get the food boxes," said Dad, heading back to the car for two wooden cupboards.

My sisters and I finished washing the dishes and left them to it.

"I love it here," I said, climbing into a big tree with wide low branches.

"Wow, a fairy ring," said Rubella, finding a circle of huge red toadstools covered in white spots.

"There's no such thing as fairies," sniffed Antoinette, going all British again. She wandered off haughtily towards a patch of lush grass. Suddenly, she squealed with delight, "look what I found," she yelled without a trace of an English accent.

Rubella and I stared enviously, as she hoisted a cow's skull up and waved it above her head.

"I'm going to take it home and put it on my dressing table," she said, carrying it towards the car.

"You are not taking that hideous thing home," said Mum stepping in front of Antoinette, hands on her hips. Her house-proud Scottish blood was roused into fighting mode.

"Aw, why not," whined Antoinette.

"Because it is disgusting," objected Mum. "Harold can you speak!" (Code for Harold-put-your-foot down.)

## Little House in the Bush

As I watched them fight over the skull it occurred to me that Antoinette could be a princess all she liked. Underneath it all, she was as much a Viking peasant as the rest of us. Perhaps Dad's hope of toughening us into pioneers was not as impossible as I first thought.

**Wendy Hamilton**

# Walking the boundary line.

The cat hated our new lifestyle of living between properties. He did not mind Mount Tiger once he got used to it. What Shnike objected to was the car ride. He was yowling loudly now, and trying to hide under Mum's seat.

"Leave him alone," said Mum in exasperation as I thumped and banged against her chair.

In a small gap of delayed obedience, I grabbed him, hauled him out, and sat him in my lap. A car passed us and he hid his eyes in my armpit. I stroked his black fur and tried to turn him over to tickle his white tummy, but he let me know loud and clear that he was not having any of that! I let him go with a yelp, and he dived back under Mum's seat.

"I told you to leave him alone," said Mum, twisting

## Little House in the Bush

in her seat and giving me a hard look. She handed me a tissue and I wiped the blood off my hand. The long scratch matched the others on my arms. Antoinette and Rubella also bore scratches on their arms and legs. Battles scars that told of the many skirmishes between a feisty cat and pesky kids. During the day he could not be bothered with us. But at night he howled under our bedroom windows and got chummy when we smuggled him into our beds.

Mum let him stay inside at night in the little house in the bush because she did not care about cat hairs on our sleeping bags. Moreover, night in the bush was scary; the cat was scared to go out after dark and so were we.

Without street lights it was pitch black. Moreover, big bush rats scurried about, *[4]morepork's hooted, and possums fought with raspy screeches. Dad, alone, stepped out into the thick blackness bravely. He was the only one who was not afraid.

"It's a lovely night, come out and look at the stars," he said, sucking in deep breaths of pure air.

I cautiously put my foot out the door and left the yellow glow of the kerosene lantern reluctantly.

"Look, there is the Southern Cross," said Dad, pointing up into the starry sky.

I quickened my pace, curious to see what he was pointing at.

---

[4] The morepork is a small brown owl found throughout New Zealand know for it distinct "morepork" call.

# Wendy Hamilton

*Mum let the cat stay in at night*

## Little House in the Bush

"And there is the Milky Way," he said, sweeping his outstretched arm over his head in an arc.

"Where?" said Antoinette, pushing past me. "There," said Dad, "and those stars over there are the Scorpion, see the tail."

We clustered around him trying to join the dots into mental pictures. By now, even Mum had joined the group, only Shnike remained cowering on the bed. It was all very nice, a real make-a-memory moment, until a possum screeched in a tree close by. That was the end of it. Everyone (except Dad) screamed and sprinted back to the lantern and the cat. Dad sighed and followed us to the shack. It was hard being the only male at times. He pulled the door closed shutting out the bush, and immediately everything felt safe. I snuggled into my sleeping bag and was soon asleep.

We awoke at dawn to the bird chorus. Mum (hoping to get a whole day reading) set out breakfast early while we played with the cat. Dad dropped his bombshell while we were eating cornflakes.

"After breakfast we will walk the boundary line."

"Couldn't we just admire it from the distance, Dear?" said Mum, eyeing the rugged wilderness doubtfully in the dawn light. She was a city girl who loathed the bush.

"Nonsense! You'll Love it," said Dad, the pride of ownership glowing in his eyes. "It will only take a couple of hours."

"We could go after the dishes are done," agreed Mum, thinking she could whisk around the fence line and still spend the bulk of the day reading.

"Aw do I have to come," I said reluctantly (I also was planning to spend the day lounging on my bed reading.)

Antoinette and Rubella did not want to go either.

"Yes, you do, you kids are not going to spend the whole day stinking inside," said Mum frowning, "it's high time you had more exercise."

"I'll dig a hole and empty the toilet," said Dad looking at Mum, "while you make a picnic lunch."

"I thought you said it will only take a couple of hours to go around the boundary."

"It will, but it is good to take a snack."

Mum nodded and went to get the bread.

"I can't be bothered going," I grumbled, as I washed the dishes in cold water. "I wanted to read David Copperfield."

"Meagan loaned me a stack of Disney comics," said Antoinette, drying a cup and giving it to Rubella, "I planned to spend the day looking at them."

"Ooh cool, can I read them too?" asked Rubella, putting it in the crockery bucket.

"Only if you don't bend them," said Antoinette generously, as we shook our sleeping bags flat. "I have to give them back."

Once the chores were done (and because there was no way of delaying it any longer) we pulled on jackets and gumboots and walked into the bush. Dad, carrying the lunch in a knapsack, led the way.

## Little House in the Bush

"A funny couple of hours," grumbled a hot and dishevelled Antoinette three hours later as we struggled down the first leg of the fence line.

"We would have been a lot further along if it weren't for that silly cat," said Mum, "I warned you it was a mistake to get a kitten but nobody listened to me."

The rest of us ignored Mum's outburst. Ten years was a long time to hold a grudge against the cat. He trailed a distance behind us, howling loudly.

"We should have locked him in the shack, like I suggested," I said.

"I'm not having him widdling under the bed," said Mum, "it's almost impossible to get the smell of cat's wee out of things."

"Pick him up, someone," said Dad in exasperation, as we backtracked for the tenth time to rescue him from a lost-in-the-bush experience. The idea was good in theory. The problem was, as soon as we went to get him, he turned around and scampered back the way we had come.

"I think he's trying to herd us out of the bush," puffed Rubella, as we ran after him.

"Yeah," I agreed, making a dive at him and catching his back legs. We had a short tussle during which he added several more scratches to my arms before surrendering.

"What are we going to do with that stupid animal?" asked Mum.

"Here, hold him for a minute," I said giving him

to Antoinette, "I've had an idea." I took off my jacket, zipped it up and tied the waist into a knot. "Shove him through the neck hole," I said, "holding out my makeshift bag so Antoinette could put Shnike in it.

He rewarded our efforts by lashing out with sixty paws and a hundred claws. When we got him contained, I tied the arms of the jacket together and slung it around my neck.

"You look like one of those African mothers in the National Geographic," giggled Antoinette.

"I do not! They look rude."

"I don't mean like that! I mean you are carrying your baby on your back through the jungle."

"Do they have jungle in Africa?" asked Rubella. "I only remember pictures of brown land and mud huts."

"This is bush not jungle," I said. "Jungles have snakes, and parrots, and plants that can eat you. There are no snakes in New Zealand."

"It looks more like jungle than an English wood," said Antoinette.

She was right about that. Tall pongas[5], lofty palms, and huge gnarled trees pushed their way up through the dense scrub and filmy ferns. Dad fired with enthusiasm, educated us as we stumbled over hidden rocks, fell down landslides, and slid on our bottoms down cliffs.

"That is a ponga," he said pointing to a fern growing high above our heads, that is a Nikou palm and this big old tree is a Rimu."

---

5    Tree ferns found throughout New Zealand

## Little House in the Bush

Shnike was not impressed. He yowled dismally on my back throughout the whole lesson. Finally, after four hours of crawling, falling, slipping, and sliding, a battered and bruised party arrived at the bottom boundary, marked by a river.

"Now wasn't that worth it!" exclaimed Dad waving at the wide expanse of shallow water flowing like liquid glass over a pebbled river bed.

"Maybe," we thought, looking at the beautiful scenery as we eased our aching bodies onto the ground.

"Well at least it's a nice place for lunch," said Mum taking the knapsack from Dad. She pulled out a packet of thick sandwiches and handed them around.

We listened to the babbling water and watched a small bird as it flitted about.

"See the way he opens his tail like a fan," whispered Dad, motioning us to sit still, "he's a Fantail."

"He's very close," I whispered.

"That's because our movement is stirring up bugs."

"I can't see any," whispered Rubella.

"That's because they are tiny, he uses his tail to change directions quickly so he can catch flying bugs."

We stared at the little bird, fascinated.

Suddenly, Shnike popped his head out of my jacket and howled loudly.

The Fantail flicked his tail in and disappeared in a flash.

"Does anyone want a drink," said Dad in his normal voice, as Antoinette pushed Shnike down and covered him with the hood of my jacket once more.

"Oh yes," we chorused, hoping for orage drink.

"Nothing like a drink of pure New Zealand mountain water," he said, taking a cup out of the knapsack and dipping it in the stream."

"Ooh yuck," squealed Antoinette, "I'm not drinking that!"

"There are many countries in the world where it is not safe to drink the water from streams, but you can here." Dad took a sip. "We are lucky to live in such a clean green country."

We eyed him doubtfully as he tipped his head back and drank.

"Delicious, pure enough to bottle up and sell in the supermarket." He rinsed the cup in the flowing water. "Who wants to be next?"

"Did you bring any orange flavouring," I asked.

"Orange flavouring!" Dad's eyebrows flew up. "You don't want to ruin the taste of pure mountain water. Here Anne, try some," he said, "dipping the cup into the water and handing it to Mum.

Mum was hot, thirsty, and she did not want to disappoint her husband, but still she hesitated.

"Go on, try it," encouraged Dad.

She took a small sip.

"How was that?" he asked, with the air of a cook watching a judge sampling pie.

"Good," said Mum, looking surprised. She took another sip more boldly and then drained the cup.

# Little House in the Bush

*The cat followed us into the bush*

## Wendy Hamilton

Mum's bravery gave the rest of us courage, and we all drank, even Antoinette. Dad was right, it was good; crystal clear and ice-cold with the merest taste of pebbles. It was not until we found the dead goat floating in the water upstream that we decided it was disgusting. "What a lot of fuss about nothing," said Dad, skirting the fly-blown carcass as we sloshed our way along the stream.

"Oh Harold, we might all get sick," said Mum horrified.

"We'll be fine," said Dad. "If you are worried just have a drink of cider vinegar when we get back. That will kill any bugs."

"I know I was adopted," moaned Antoinette. "My real family would not drink dead-goat water."

"Don't be silly," said Mum, glaring at her.

I said nothing as I walked around the goat because I was preoccupied with an even bigger problem. The cat, hearing us splash through the stream, struggled on my back. Suddenly, he decided to make a bold bid for freedom. He shot a paw out, dug his claws like grappling hooks into my neck and thrust his head out of the hood.

"Hold on to him or we will lose him forever down here," screamed Antoinette and Rubella, leaping on me and pushing him back down. I climbed out of the stream with my neck bleeding and continued the journey on the riverbank. For a long time, we traipsed on, one foot after the other, until we came to a steep little creek that fed into the stream.

## Little House in the Bush

"Up here," said Dad, turning into it. A small trickle of water dribbled between large boulders that rose in a rugged stairway. It was hard going crawling uphill on all fours like long-legged crabs. For me, however, it had its rewards; the cat had settled down. Only the steady howling indicated he was still alive. I suggested someone else might like to carry him the last leg of the journey, but strangely, nobody was keen.

"Oh Harold, how much further are we going," moaned Mum. "This has been much longer than two hours and you didn't tell me I'd be climbing Everest."

"Not much longer," lied Dad.

We kept climbing until we reached the top of the staircase. There we found the Old Man. Not the type found in old folk's homes, he was, in fact, an ancient and very majestic Rimu tree, growing on a cliff high above us. He clung by his toes to the edge of a tall waterfall that fell into the basin of sparkling water at our feet.

"Oh!" breathed Mum, awestruck. "It's worth all that revolting tea-tree and nightmare land to own this little piece of heaven."

"Actually," coughed Dad uncomfortably, "this bit belongs to the Reserve, that's our piece over there." He pointed through the trees to a scrubby blighted patch.

It was dark by the time we finally staggered out of the bush onto the grassy plateau of home. Antoinette and Rubella flopped onto the ground while I lifted the jacket-bag off my back and zipped it open. As soon as the cat's feet were free, he shot into the shack and hid under the bed. Meanwhile, Mum (drooping with exhaustion) scratched together a quick dinner before collapsing on her bunk. Dad sitting on a campstool, read the newspaper by the light of the lantern. 'Coast to Coast Iron Man a Real Challenge,' said the front-page headline in bold letters.

"Huh!" snorted Dad, puffing out his chest with pride. "Those blokes don't know the meaning of an Iron Man until they have walked our boundary line."

**Little House in the Bush**

# Cattle

"The grass is getting very long at Mount Tiger," said Dad, one evening.

"Shh, The Dick Van Dyke Show is about to begin," said Mum, sitting down in her armchair and putting her feet up on a footstool. She picked up her knitting as the music faded away and Mary Tyler Moore walked on screen.

"I'm thinking of buying cattle," continued Dad.

"Cows!" said Mum, dropping a stitch.

I squirmed in my chair and wished I was an adult and could tell them to shut up, it was hard to hear the television over their talking.

"No," said Dad.

"That's good," said Mum, picking up the stitch and turning her attention back to the show.

"Steers."

"What are steers?" asked Mum with one eye on the

screen and one on Dad.

"Castrated bulls," said Dad.

Now he had all of our attention. The crunch line of the first gag passed unnoticed by any of us.

"Bulls!" quavered Mum shocked.

"Bulls?" Antoinette, Rubella, and I echoed

"No, not bulls, steers."

"Is a steer a lady cow or a man cow?" asked Rubella. It was a good question and we held our breath as we waited for Dad's answer.

"A man," said Dad.

"Then they are bulls!" Mum threw her knitting down and her lips went thin. "I don't mind living in the bush on weekends and school holidays, Harold, but I draw the line at bulls!"

At this, Rubella started crying, and Antoinette muttered about being adopted and how her real family would not mess around with bulls. I also was horrified. I loved our little house in the bush and the colour red. The thought of wearing green while I crept around a paddock full of ferocious bulls was awful.

"They are boy cows with the bull part taken away," explained Dad patiently, in terms we could understand. "Steers are gentle."

Four females with crossed arms glared at him. None of us were convinced.

"Here, I'll prove it to you," said Dad. He disappeared into the hallway and rattled about in the cupboard at the top of the staircase where the tin of important papers

## Little House in the Bush

lived. While he was away the rest of us turned back to the Dick Van Dyke Show halfheartedly. We did not care that we had missed the first half of the show, our minds were grappling with a bigger problem than the fake troubles on television.

"See," said Dad, coming back into the room. He had open in his hand a small book containing his family history. He held it up. "Here is your pioneering great-great-uncle with his team of oxen."

We crowded around and looked at the faded page. A man with a bushy beard and wearing his Sunday suit (for the camera) posed beside two oxen hitched to a homemade cart, on which two children sat. The caption underneath said, Robert Johnson taking his children to school on his oxen cart.

"The oxen look very big." Mum was still unconvinced.

"They won't be fully grown ones like that, I want weaners," said Dad, "they will be little more than Bobby calves. We will fatten them and sell them for a profit."

"Bobby calves!" I said, thinking I could wear my red jacket after all.

"Bobby calves are so cute!" said Rubella perking up.

"Remember the ones at the Agricultural and Pastoral show?" said Antoinette, imagining herself winning a blue ribbon and showing it to all her friends.

"Well, we did buy the land hoping to make a bit of extra money from it," said Mum giving in.

# Wendy Hamilton

The closing music blared out of the television. We had missed the whole Dick Van Dyke Show, but it did not matter. We were all excited about getting calves.

"I'll give the Stock and Station Agent a call in the morning and get him to look out for some for me," said Dad, "there is a cattle sale on Wednesday."

That Friday evening, when we arrived at Mount Tiger there were fourteen steers in the paddock.

"They look healthy," nodded Dad approvingly as he got out of the car.

"What's that one," I asked pointing to a red-brown beast who stood out among all the other black and white bodies.

"He's a Hereford," said Dad inspecting the herd. The calves huddled tightly together and stared at us with big soft eyes.

"They are so cute," said Antoinette, without a trace of the British accent.

"They are adorable," I agreed, advancing towards them slowly with my hand outstretched.

Even Mum thought they were alright. Rubella (carrying Shnike) was the last to get out of the car. She wandered over to us and put him on the ground. The calves instantly switched their attention from us to the cat. They stretched their necks towards him and sniffed curiously. The cat sank his belly low to the ground and froze in terror as the calves took a step forward. That was when Shnike made his big mistake. He shot off, and headed straight for the shack. The steers (with the

## Little House in the Bush

friskiness of youth) threw up their tails and galloped after him, stopping only when he streaked under the building and disappeared from sight. In the morning Shnike stayed on the highest bunk while us kids went forth to tame the monsters.

"Here boys," said Rubella, advancing slowly with a fist full of long grass. The fattest one (with a black marking splashed across his white face) stopped ripping up grass with his tongue and stretched out his neck hesitatingly.

"That one looks as if a cow pooped on his face," giggled Antoinette.

"Yeah, he does." Now we were all laughing, "let's call him Poopsy," I said.

The suggestion seemed good to the others.

"And that one is Horus," said Antoinette, pointing to the red Hereford.

"He's got little horns," I said, fascinated.

While Rubella inched towards Poopsy, we named the rest.

"He's thinking about taking it," I said, turning my attention back to Poopsy. Rubella stretched forward and touched his nose with the grass, but the steer changed his mind at the last moment and ambled off.

"I've got an idea," said Antoinette, running back to the shack. She fossicked in the food cupboard and found a carrot. "Where are you going with that?" asked Mum, reading her mind, "you're not feeding carrots to those calves!"

# Wendy Hamilton

*The steers galloped after the cat*

## Little House in the Bush

Antoinette could be cute and charming when she chose. She looked at Mum with a friendly, cheeky grin.

"Aw please, just one?"

"I suppose so," said Mum caving in.

"Thanks Mum," said Antoinette, scampering back to us. "Here boy," she said, holding out the carrot. It was an inspired idea. Poopsy took several steps forward, craned his neck and licked the carrot into his mouth.

"Ooo, that feels like sandpaper," giggled Antoinette, as his raspy tongue slipped across her fingers.

"I wish we had more carrots," said Rubella enviously, "that one over there wants one."

"You're right," said Antoinette, "he looks funny with his tongue sticking out. I wonder where we can get more carrots."

"Jane gets old carrots from the supermarket for her horse," I said, having a brainwave. "They throw them out and she gets them free, I could see if I can get some."

The others thought that was a good idea, so on Thursday after school, I rode my bike around to the back of the supermarket, past several big refrigerated trucks to an open garage door. Men were bustling about shifting boxes. I spied a fatherly man throwing squishy tomatoes into a dumpster.

"Excuse me," I said politely, "I wondered if you are throwing away any carrots that I could have?"

"Sure love, are they for your horse?" he asked kindly.

"No, pet calves," I said.

## Wendy Hamilton

"Well, that's a new one," he laughed, "wait here." He disappeared into the building and came back carrying a banana box full of bagged carrots.

"Here you go," he said dumping it on the carrier behind the seat of my bike. I stretched two bungee cords over the box and wobbled it to make sure it would not fall off.

"Thanks a lot," I said, putting my foot on the peddle and riding off.

The bribery worked like magic. In this way, the Boys (as we fondly called them) became exceedingly tame. They mooed whenever they saw us, hoping for a carrot or a friendly scratch. They especially liked us scratching the base of their tails.

"Just look at Poopsy," laughed Antoinette, as the fat bullock stretched his neck up and rocked from side to side in ecstasy. Dad, nearby, paused in his labour of planting trees to admire the glossy steer.

"That's a beautiful beast," he said with pride, look how big he has grown in such a short time. "He's a natural forager."

"He is too much of a natural forager," said Mum grimly, "just look at my washing!" She held up a white shirt with green arms and a mangled tea-towel. "I washed these by hand this morning and hung them on the fence to dry. Look what that naughty beast did when my back was turned. I had to pull them out of his mouth!"

"That's nothing," I giggled. "He tried to eat the hood

# Little House in the Bush

of my jacket. What made it worse was I was wearing it at the time."

"Ha, ha," laughed Dad, "who had a keen sense of humour.

"I don't see anything to laugh about," said Mum, who did not.

Dad had a change of heart a week later when he discovered Poopsy on the wrong side of the electric fence eating the last of his seedlings.

"Five hundred trees!" he said sadly, "he's eaten five hundred trees. If he keeps on like that, he will be at the butcher's quicker than I intended,"

The butcher! That was an alarming thought.

"Please don't send him to the butcher, Dad," we pleaded, bursting into tears. "We love the boys."

"They will have to go one day," said Mum hardheartedly.

"But we won't be the ones to send them," said Dad relenting. "When they get big enough, I'll sell them and someone else can finish fattening them for the works."

"Oh, thank you, thank you, Daddy," we said, throwing our arms around him. Dad grinned; he was as fond of the boys as we were. "And next time I won't rely on a flimsy little electric fence to keep a natural forager away from a banquet."

**Wendy Hamilton**

# Short on Grass

The rain dropped over Mount Tiger in a heavy curtain as the mist in the valley rose to meet it. Four of us were cooped up in the shack. A six-foot cube is a small space, even for a family with troll ancestors. Antoinette and Rubella sat on the middle bunk playing cards.

"I win," shouted Antoinette, throwing an ace down.

"No, you don't," shouted Rubella, going red in the face (she was very competitive and hated to lose at anything) "you didn't say 'Last Card.'"

"I did too, you weren't listening," shouted Antoinette. "I won that fair and square, Rubella!"

"No, you didn't," said Rubella, sitting upright hurriedly. "Ow," she yelped as she hit her head on the bottom of my bunk.

I leaned over the edge of the bed and hung my head down. "Shut up you two," I shouted, "I'm trying to

## Little House in the Bush

read."

"That's it," said Mum from the opposite bunk. She shut her book with a bang. "Get your gumboots and raincoats on and go outside.

"Do I have to," I moaned, "I wasn't part of the fight."

"I heard you shouting too," said Mum unmoved.

We grumbled as we pulled raincoats off the hook on the door and dragged gumboots out from under the bottom bunk. The rain eased as we stepped reluctantly out the door.

"I'm going to see if there are any frogs," said Antoinette, sloshing through the mud towards the spring. "Do you want to come, Wend?"

"Nah," I said, "I can't be bothered."

"I'll come," said Rubella, running after her.

I wandered over to Dad. He was busy tightening a sagging fence.

"How long is it going to keep raining?" I asked.

"Only the Good Lord knows the answer to that one," said Dad. The fence creaked and straightened as he pumped the wire-strainers back and forth. "It's June so it can last for weeks." He re-fastened the end and twanged the taut wire. "That's better," he said, brushing the rain off his face. He straightened up and stared at the pasture thoughtfully. "If this weather goes on much longer, we will run out of grass."

"Mr. Carrington's cows have less to eat than our boys," I said, comparing the fields on either side of the boundary.

## Wendy Hamilton

"He likes to run his stock hard," said Dad. "I admit it's better for the land to keep cattle lean, because then they will eat all the weeds and rubbish. But I could never do it. I just can't bear to see an animal hungry." (That was typical of Dad. He was a kind man with a soft heart.)

"I thought the rain was good for the grass," I said puzzled.

"Not in winter," said Dad, "it's too cold."

"But it doesn't snow in Northland."

"I know, but it's still too cold for grass to grow, and the cattle pug up the ground with their feet. If it doesn't stop soon, I will have to put them down in the bush. There is a lot of fodder in that back paddock."

I pulled a face. "Won't they get lost, there are hardly any fences down there?"

"If they stay within calling distance, we'll be alright."

Dad had a solid basis for his confidence. Like the Pied Piper, wherever he went the boys were sure to follow; at least as far as the fences allowed. As soon as they saw him striding about in his beanie hat and gumboots, they sent out a chorus of mooing, as they kicked up their heels and frisked behind him. Even now, they were standing on the other side of the fence watching him work.

"Moo," said Poopsy, staring at him intensely. As if it were a signal, all the rest started mooing.

"You boys want a new paddock, do you?" said Dad.

## Little House in the Bush

"Oh, all right, there's nothing for it, I'll have to put them down the back." He threw the wire-strainers into a bucket of fence staples.

"Come on, come on," he shouted, walking beside the fence. When they heard this, the commotion doubled as they followed him in a shuffling crocodile line. At the top of a small rise stood a gate. He swung it open and stepped to the side quickly.

"Look at them go," I laughed, as they poured through the gap and careered about the field, butting heads and leaping upon each other.

"This will make them happy," said Dad, shutting the gate and hooking the latch. "I'll go ahead and open the gates. You go behind them and shoo along any stragglers." He lifted his voice and called, "come on, come on," as he moved away.

"Hurry up boys," I shouted, waving my arms.

They stopped fooling about and trotted after Dad, who led them through another gate, up over the ridge and down into the bush. I lost sight of them as the dense foliage opened its mouth and swallowed them.

When we got back, Antoinette and Rubella had given up looking for frogs, and were fighting over a game of snakes and ladders.

"I want to go home," said Mum, "this is an impossible way to spend the school holidays, we need a bigger building."

"Alright," said Dad.

"Alright about what?" said Mum, "alright we can go

home or alright we can get a bigger building?"

"Both," said Dad, packing the perishable food into a basket.

**Little House in the Bush**

# The Cattle Hunt

The rain had stopped, and once again we were at Mount Tiger.

"What about this garage, Harold?" asked Mum pointing at a photo in a shiny brochure. "I think this one would be nice. (She had not forgotten the idea of bigger accommodation.)

"Hmm, looks good, "said Dad in a preoccupied tone of voice.

"You don't even have to build it, they deliver it and put it up in a day," said Mum, reading the blurb.

"It's time I got the boys up from the back paddock," said Dad, pulling on his gumboots. "If we lose them and have to buy more stock, there will be no money for a bigger building."

"Oh Harold, do you think that's possible?" said Mum in alarm.

## Wendy Hamilton

"Not really," said Dad, "but it's time I got them up."

"They will be pleased to see you," I said, "they've never been down there so long before."

"The paddocks have benefitted from a rest," said Dad, looking at the lime-green fields. "Two weeks without big feet churning the ground into mud and dry weather has done wonders."

"I'll come with you," I said, pulling on my gumboots as Dad put on his old beanie hat.

He nodded, and picked up a long stick leaning on the side of the shack. "Come on then," he said, stabbing the stick into the ground with every stride. I trotted after him through the gate, past the spring, up over the ridge, and down to the edge of the bush.

The gate between the pasture and the wilderness was a Taranaki gate. I glared at it with hatred. I had wrestled with many Taranaki gates and never left the fight without some kind of wound. This one was the usual beast; fence battens strung on the wires, like a set of taut guitar strings running through frets. It was the spring-loaded aspect of the gate that troubled me. It took eye-popping strength to unhook the latch, and the kickback (once this was accomplished) was fearsome. Dad, however, unlatched it with authority and opened it without event.

"COME ON, COME ON," he called, dragging the sagging tangle of battens and wire to the side. "That's strange," he said, pausing, "I can't hear them, they should be mooing and moving up by now." He lifted

## Little House in the Bush

his voice again. "COME ON, COME ON."

"COME ON, COME ON." I added my voice to the call and our shouts rang out over the valley, but still there was no answering reply.

"Let's walk down the ridge a little way," said Dad, frowning. "The fence down here is not too good, they might have pushed through and be down in the other paddock."

I nodded and we slipped and slithered downward as we crashed through tea tree and pig fern.

"Looks like they have broken through," said Dad coming across a large gap in the fence. He cupped his hands around his mouth and called "COME ON, COME ON."

"COME ON, COME ON," I hollered, copying him.

The wind blew our voices down the long valley out to the blue triangle of harbour in the distance, but still there was no answer.

"They must be a long way down," said Dad. He took off his hat and rubbed his forehead. I kept quiet because he wore his 'thinking' face. "There's nothing for it," he said at last, putting his hat on decisively, "we need everyone for a full-scale cattle hunt."

Together we clambered back out of the bush, plodded up the hill and over the ridge, strode down the slope past the spring, and traipsed through the gate and over to the shack.

"Where are the boys?" asked Mum in alarm, when she saw we were alone.

## Wendy Hamilton

"Lost," said Dad, "I need everyone for a cattle hunt."

"Do I have to come?" whined Antoinette, looking up from her comic.

"I said everyone," said Dad. "And lock the cat in," he added, spotting Shnike on the top bunk, "we don't want him following this time."

Mum and the others pulled on gumboots and gathered around Dad, as I shut the door carefully. (I, more than the others, did not want another cat in the bush saga.)

"Everyone, take a walking stick," said Dad handing out long tea-tree sticks, "use it as a third leg on the steep bits. Let's get going."

We followed him through the gate, past the spring, up and over the ridge, and down into the bush.

"Now, I want you all to spread out in a fan and move down towards the stream, make as much noise as you can. If you get lost, head uphill, eventually you will come to the road or the forestry. We will meet down by the stream. OK?"

We nodded and spread through the bush as best we could. It was tough going. Pig Fern scratched our legs, tree roots tripped us up, Bush-Lawyer ripped us with small barbs, and patches of cutty-grass slashed our arms. The ferns grew so huge and the trees were clustered together so thickly, we quickly lost sight of each other; only the string of 'COME ONs' linked us together. After a horribly long time, we slipped and slithered down a steep bank and emerged at the edge of

## Little House in the Bush

the stream.

"They must have gone downstream," said Dad "because if they headed up the hill one of the neighbours would have found them and called us."

"Do we have to go back into the bush," I asked gloomily.

"No, we can follow the stream," said Dad, "it is easier going and our voices will carry up the hill. If they are near, they will callout."

This plan seemed good to us and we sloshed along the stream for a long, long, time. At last Dad called a halt. "They could be anywhere by now," he said. "They might have walked to Parua Bay for all we know. We better turn around and go home."

We backtracked along the riverbed, hopping from rock to rock halfheartedly.

"There's no point spreading out, stick together and follow the goat track," said Dad pointing to a bare patch running up a fold in the hill.

It took too much energy to speak, so we merely nodded, and wiped the sweat off our red faces. I splashed out of the water and climbed up the steep bank. Somewhere during the safari, I lost my walking stick, so I used the trunks of saplings to haul myself upwards. Fire ran along my calves, up to my thighs and into my buttocks, as I relentlessly plodded higher and higher; one foot after another, my heart hammering in my chest and throbbing in my head, as I sucked air in and out like a blacksmith's bellows.

## Wendy Hamilton

"Not much further to go, nearly there," shouted Dad every so often.

It was all lies, some black magic in the bush had turned our honest father into a liar. He did not speak another word of truth until we got to the Taranaki gate. Never did my old enemy look so friendly as when we staggered out of the bush. We collapsed on the grass and lay speachless while Dad shut it.

"Come on everyone," said Dad taking Mum's hand and pulling her up, "the longer you stay here the harder it will be to get moving again."

We groaned as we slowly creaked to our feet (Dad did not bother to help any of the rest of us up) and trotted after them, our legs trembling with exertion, up the hill, over the ridge, past the spring, through the gate and into the shack. The cat, disturbed by our entrance, stretched his legs and yawned leisurely.

"I wish I was a cat," I said, flopping onto my bunk as Mum put the kettle on the camp cooker.

....

We did eventually find the boys, but not with another cattle hunt in the bush. Mum put an ad in the paper and a farmer many miles away rang to say he had them.

"I'll have to hire a cattle truck to bring them home again," said Dad, when he heard where they were. "I can't see any other way of doing it."

"That sounds expensive," said Mum, chewing her lip in disappointment, "we almost had enough money for a new garage but now we won't."

## Little House in the Bush

"It will be alright," said Dad, "we will find a way around it. At least we don't have to buy more stock."

And he was right. The boys arrived home in style, and three weeks later a shiny aluminium garage was delivered and erected at Mount Tiger.

**Wendy Hamilton**

# A Bigger Little House in the Bush

Dad drove the car and trailer, past the little house and through the gate that led to our small quarry.

"Oh Harold, you'll get the wheels bogged if you turn off the gravel," protested Mum. "Leave the car here, it's not far to walk."

"I suppose so," said Dad, pulling to a stop. He twisted in his seat and looked us in the eye, "I know you are all excited about the new garage, but before you all rush off, everybody is to take something with them, I don't want to see anyone walking without something in their hand."

"Alright," we chorused, as we tumbled out and Dad loosened the ropes on the trailer.

"And keep away from the edge of the paddock, the

## Little House in the Bush

drop down to the quarry is dangerous," added Mum.

I nodded, took the spade Dad handed me and skipped up the small rise to our bigger little house.

The side door rattled with a tinny hollow sound as Dad twisted the doorknob and pushed it open.

"This is more like it!" said Mum, twirling in the middle of the room, "finally, space to move."

"I've never seen a shed with a grassy floor before," said Antoinette, looking at the ground in surprise.

"Why are the windows so high?" said Rubella, jumping up and down as she tried in vain to see out.

"And why is there a big gap all around the bottom," I asked.

"It is designed to have a concrete floor," said Dad, dropping a heavy roll of black polythene on the ground, and hoisting open the large garage door; it slid up smoothly and lay like a flat shelf above my head.

"Will we be able to see out the windows when we get the floor?" asked Rubella.

"Yes and no," said Dad, "yes you could see out the windows but no, we are not getting a floor, we spent the money on trucking the boys home."

"No floor!" Antoinette spoke as if she had a marble in her mouth as she played the part of a shocked aristocrat.

The rest of us peasants ignored her outburst.

"That's a nice view," said Mum looking out at the grassy hill opposite. "I don't often see the ridge from this angle. It's hard to believe the land drops away so steeply at the side."

## Wendy Hamilton

"It is a good spot," agreed Dad, looking at a small stand of trees in the bottom of the shallow valley, "nice and close to the spring, that will make carrying water easier."

"Carrying water!" said Lady Antoinette, even more outraged. "Why can't we be like other people, none of my friends have to carry water or live in a grass hut that the possums can get in."

"Don't be silly," said Mum sharply, "Dad will put some boards around the bottom, and I brought an old carpet square to put on the ground."

"But the carpet will get damp," I said, thinking through the practicalities.

"No, it won't," said Dad, tapping the roll of polythene with his foot. "I'll lay polythene down first."

I nodded, "that will work, it will be like a tent floor."

"We need to have dinner and get settled for the night before we lose the light," said Mum, noticing the shadows lengthen.

"Right," said Dad, "come on everyone, leave the bigger things on the trailer overnight, but we'll unload the tools now. That will give us ahead start tomorrow morning."

"Ahead start, for what?" asked Antoinette, her eyes narrowing.

"For turfing the floor," said Dad, "I need help to get all the grass removed."

"Work!" spat Antoinette, pulling a face. "I knew it wouldn't be anything fun. I wish you had let me go to

## Little House in the Bush

Meagan's place for the weekend, she doesn't have to work."

"It's good you knew what to expect," said Mum hardheartedly, "and you are part of this family whether you like it or not."

"Well, I don't like it," said Antoinette, stomping off to collect her share of the tools.

We started work early the next morning and by the end of the weekend, the bigger little-house was livable. Once the gap around the bottom was covered in, and the carpet rolled over the polythene, it felt quite cosy. Rubella and I sat on the floor playing knucklebones, while Mum arranged a motley assortment of chairs around a rickety table.

"I'm glad that's over," said Antoinette, slumping into an old armchair with a busted spring in the seat. She blew air onto the blisters on her hands, "digging turf is as hard as carrying water."

I fumbled and dropped a knucklebone.

"My turn," said Rubella.

I handed them to her. "I like my new bed," I said, looking at the bunks Dad had made out of wobbly tea-tree trunks and wire-wove bed-bases.

"I don't see why you got the top bed," said Antoinette in a peeved tone.

"There have to be some privileges for being the eldest," I said pulling rank.

"I still think it would have been fairer to flip a coin," said Antoinette.

## Wendy Hamilton

"Let's draw straws," said Rubella, "then I can be in it too."

"No," said Antoinette, not wishing to risk getting Rubella's bed. Even a bottom bunk was more exciting than a boring single bed.

"You could make it into a fourposter bed," I said, picking up a curtain lying on Mum and Dad's double bed by the opposite wall.

"Ooh, that's a great idea," said Antoinette seizing it and tucking the top under my mattress so it hung down.

"Oh no you don't," said Mum, pausing in her work, "that's mine, I want a bit of privacy. It goes there," she pointed to a curtain wire running along the bottom of a ceiling truss, "I just haven't got around to putting it up yet."

"I might have known," said Antoinette, dumping it back on the double bed.

"Once you finish installing the sink bench, Harold, I will feel quite civilized," said Mum, changing the subject.

"Ooh, does that mean we are getting running water," asked Antoinette, her eyes lighting up.

We all looked expectantly at Dad, water-carrying was heavy hard work.

"Maybe one day, but not for a while," he said, dashing our hopes. He crawled out from under the makeshift cabinet. "Wendy, come over here, I'm going outside to sort out the drainage, when you see a pipe come through the wall, grab it and pull it up to the sink outlet."

"OK, Dad." I bent down and stared at the hole until a fat green hose slid through it. "Got it, I yelled pulling it through.

"I can take it from here," said Dad, coming back inside. "You kids go and get some water so I can see if I need to dig a longer trench." He pointed to a stack of buckets.

We picked them up reluctantly, and sloped out of the door with hunched shoulders and hangdog expressions. We got back in time to see Dad whack two four-gallon drums on the end of the bench. They were made of heavy plastic, a vile shade of orange, and had a small tap on the bottom.

"Tip it in here," said Dad, taking Rubella's bucket and emptying it into the wide mouth of a drum before giving it back to her.

We did as we were told. Meanwhile, Dad twiddled with the tap. As soon as a thin stream of water flowed into the sink, he rushed outside.

"Is it working?" called Mum.

"Nearly," shouted Dad, "I just need to slope the ditch a little more." We heard the soft thuds of his spade as he fixed the problem. At length he called, "you can turn the tap off now, Wendy, we don't want to waste water."

I twisted the handle of the little tap and the water stopped flowing.

"I think I will sew a curtain to cover the shelves," said Mum, stacking pans and plates under the sink bench. "I've got a floral sheet I can use."

"Good idea," said Dad coming in. He climbed on the table and knocked a four-inch nail into the rafter above it. "Pass me the Tilly lamp, someone."

Antoinette handed it to him and he hung it on the nail.

"Not bad for a weekend's work," he said, climbing down. He glanced at his watch and sighed. "What a pity tomorrow is Monday, it's time to go home."

**Little House in the Bush**

# Antoinette's Bedroom

Friday night rolled around quickly and once again we were at Mount Tiger. Dad twisted the key and pushed open the door of the bigger little house.

"Pooh, what's that smell?" said Mum, sniffing the air.

"Ooh yuck, it's horrible," said Antoinette lifting her arm and burying her nose in the crook of her elbow.

"It seems to be coming from the floor," said Rubella, who was the shortest and therefore the closest to the ground.

Dad walked over to the corner by the big garage door and lifted the carpet. Then he peeled back the polythene. Lying like cream squiggles on the brown earth were hundreds of dead worms.

## Wendy Hamilton

"I think I'm going to be sick," said Antoinette, rushing out the door.

"Harold, how are we going to get rid of them? It's like having a mortuary in our basement," said Mum, looking appalled, "as Dad replaced the polythene and dropped the carpet back into place.

"What's a mortuary?" asked Rubella.

"A place where they keep dead people," I said, in my best Frankenstein imitation.

Rubella, pretending to be frightened, squealed and hid behind Mum.

"Don't be silly, Wendy," said Mum, glaring at me. "Say sorry to your sister for frightening her."

Rubella leaned to the side and poked her tongue out at me slyly.

"She's poking her t…"

"I don't want to hear," said Mum holding up her hand. "Wendy, say sorry to your sister."

"Sorry," I mumbled.

"That's better," said Mum.

Rubella lowered the hoods of her eyes and smirked at me.

"How are we going to get rid of them, Harold?" said Mum, turning back to the worm problem.

"We don't have to," said Dad, "the smell will disappear as the floor dries and packs down."

"I'm not sleeping in here with dead worms and all the rest of you," said Antoinette, popping her head through the door, "I'm going to sleep in the shack."

## Little House in the Bush

"Alright," said Dad.

"Oh, Harold, I'm not happy about that, it's too far away!

"It's not far, I could throw a rock and hit it."

"She's only twelve and the lock is a bent wire."

"It is perfectly safe out here."

"I know, but I still don't like it."

"I'll tell you what, Antoinette," said Dad giving in, "sleep in here tonight, and tomorrow we will shift the shack behind the garage so you can have your own bedroom."

"Alright," said Antoinette, taking long leaps on the tip of her toes to her bed. "The stink will be worth it to have my own room."

As always, Dad was a man of his word. After breakfast he assembled us around the builder's shed.

"We are not going to dismantle the shed this time," he said, laying two lines of fence posts on the ground next to the shack. "We are going to move it the same way your great, great, grandfather shifted his house."

"Was it a little house like this?" asked Rubella.

"No, it was a proper family home," said Dad, laying out another line of posts.

"Why did they shift it?" I said.

"The land they built it on was infertile and all their crops couldn't grow, so they rolled the house down to better land," said Dad, sliding the fourth row of posts under one end of the shed. He straightened up. "Everyone come around this side and lift when I say.

## Wendy Hamilton

Then Rubella, I want you to pull the blocks out from under the corners, got it."

We nodded and mumbled a few doubtful yeses as Dad jammed a long metal bar into the gap under the building.

"One, two, three, lift."

Dad swung down on his bar, while the rest of us almost wrenched our arms from their sockets as we pulled upwards.

"NOW, Rubella!" gasped Dad.

Rubella dragged the two concrete blocks out of the way clumsily.

"Right, let her down onto the poles."

We lowered the shed carefully and let go with relief.

"Do the same again with this end," said Dad, carrying his metal bar around to the other side.

Once again, we lifted, and once again, Rubella dragged the corner blocks out of the way. "Good job," Dad said, "now keep this end off the ground and push.

We pushed and strained, and the building moved forward onto the second row of poles.

"That's good, keep the momentum going," shouted Dad as the little house slid onto the next set of poles. When it passed onto the third row, Dad let go and rushed around to the front. "Keep it coming," he called, as he quickly laid out another line of posts.

The first row of posts peeped out from under the building. As we stepped over them, Dad ran back, gathered them up and ran around to the front again.

## Little House in the Bush

"That's it, keep coming," he yelled, laying the posts out rapidly.

We stepped over another line of posts. As if by magic, Dad appeared behind us once again, scooped up the posts and disappeared around the front. In this way, we trundled the shed along the track that led to the quarry, and through the gate.

"OK, Stop," said Dad, once we were clear of the big puriri tree that grew next to the gate. "We need to swivel the shed ninety degrees."

"What does ninety degrees mean?" asked Rubella, who had not got to that math's unit yet.

"Facing the garage, Dummy," said Antoinette, who had. The next few minutes were an awful sequence of lifting and shuffling as Dad directed the tricky operation and swiveled the posts under the shed.

"How are we going to get it over the ditch?" I asked, looking at the grassy culvert running alongside the track.

"I'll make a bridge," said Dad, picking up a spade that leaned against the trunk of the Puriri tree. "You can rest for a few minutes."

We slumped on the ground, grateful for the respite. All too soon, however, posts spanned the gap and Dad marshalled his troops once again.

"OK everyone, PUSH," he commanded.

We heaved and strained, and slowly the little house creaked over the bridge, crept up the small rise, and came to rest beside the bigger little house.

# Wendy Hamilton

*We pushed, and the building moved forward*

## Little House in the Bush

"I'm glad that's over," said Mum, leaning against the wall and wiping the sweat off her forehead. Antoinette, Rubella, and I made loud sounds of agreement.

"Not quite," said Dad, "I will need a bit of help to lift it back onto the foundations."

Our faces fell and our shoulders drooped.

"I'll go and get the concrete blocks," he continued, "while you put the kettle on Mother, it's morning tea time."

We perked up at the idea of morning tea. Dad took the wheelbarrow and went off to collect the blocks as Mum went inside and lit the primus stove. Antoinette opened the door of her new bedroom and us three girls danced about on the sloping floor. By the time Dad got all the blocks, Mum had made a pot of tea and mixed up a jug of orange drink for us kids.

"Come and get it," she called, lifting the garage door open.

We stopped dancing and rushed around the corner into the garage.

"Pooh, it still smells in here," said Antoinette, taking a cup. "I'm going to eat mine outside."

"That's a good idea," said Mum. She handed Rubella an old blanket. "Spread this under a tree, Rubella. Antoinette, take the teapot, I'll bring the cups." She handed me a packet of animal biscuits, "you can all have two biscuits as a special treat."

We did as we were told and flumped down on the blanket. Dad tipped the concrete blocks out of his wheelbarrow and joined us, as Mum poured the tea and handed him a packet of boring crackers.

Our biscuits were far more exciting. I hunted through the bag for a lion.

"Don't finger them all," admonished Mum, "just pick one off the top."

I tilted the bag so they fell into different positions, and peered through a cellophane window in the packaging, but still no lion.

"Can you see a camel?" asked Antoinette.

"Yeah," I said, offering the mouth of the bag to her carefully.

Antoinette took out an orange camel and a pink rhinoceros. I shook the bag gently, hoping to spot a lion.

"Do you want a hippopotamus as usual?" I asked Rubella, as a green one rose to the surface.

"Ooh yes," said Rubella. She took it and a purple horse.

I shook the bag again and two yellow lions popped up. I smiled, took them, and twisted the bag shut.

The next few minutes were quiet as we licked all the icing off; it was unthinkable to eat an animal biscuit any other way. The ritual was always the same. Once the icing was gone, we ate the tail (if there was one) then the legs (one by one.) If there were ears, they went before the head, and the head went before the neck, and finally we ate the body. It was a lengthy process and two animal biscuits took even longer, but eventually, all the animals were slaughtered and gone.

## Little House in the Bush

"Time to get back to work," said Dad, standing up and brushing crumbs off his trousers, as Mum folded the blanket and popped it back into the garage. I licked my fingers and trailed after them. Once again, we assembled around the shed and hoisted it up and dropped it down at Dad's command. Getting the blocks in place and the floor level was fiddly work, and our arms were aching and our tempers frayed by the time Dad was satisfied, but at last it was done.

"Do I have to have all these old bunks in here?" Antoinette asked, her top lip elongating.

"No, they can all come out if you like," said Dad.

"I'd like to keep an extra one," the marble was back in my sister's mouth, and she oozed the air of one who had gone up a notch socially. "I might invite a friend to stay now I have my own pad."

I knew by the tilt of her nose that the shack had magically turned into a castle. Under the right conditions my sister's imagination soared to extraordinary heights.

"Even Meagan?" I asked wickedly.

"Antoinette's nose lowered and her lip popped back into place.

"No, not Meagan," she said, shaking her head so hard her ponytail swung. Even Antoinette's imagination had its limits.

**Wendy Hamilton**

# Antoinette's Lipstick

"It's blowing a gale out there," said Dad, staggering inside and leaning his spade against the wall. "The wind coming up the valley is strong enough to blow the hairs off a cat's back."

"Did you get all the trees planted?" asked Mum, lighting the primus stove and setting the kettle on top.

"Yeah," Dad took off his gumboots, "in a few years those little macrocarpa seedlings will be a great shelterbelt."

"I still think we need a fence along the edge of the quarry," said Mum, reaching under the skirt of the sink bench for the teapot. "Even if they grow into a thick hedge, some child might push through and tumble over the side."

"I am going to put in a fence," said Dad, padding

## Little House in the Bush

across the floor in his socks and sitting down in an old armchair, "but I'll build it this side of the trees. I'm not having the cattle eat all these seedlings as they did with the ones along the ridge."

"Good idea," said Mum, pouring a small amount of warm water from the kettle into the teapot and swilling it around, "we don't want that happening again, such a waste of money."

"And energy," agreed Dad, stretching his legs out and crossing them at the ankles.

Mum tipped the water out as a big gust whistled through a gap between the top of the wall and the eves. "This gale reminds me of when I was a child in Palmerston North," she said, as the kettle boiled, "the wind was always blowing there."

"Yeah," said Dad (who was also raised there.) "When I was a kid, we used to go to the beach at Himatangi and lean on the wind."

"It was hard riding a bike," said Mum, popping a scoop of tea into the pot and pouring hot water on top.

"Only if you were going against the wind."

"That's true," Mum laughed, taking two cups from the cupboard, "it was good when it pushed from behind." She picked up a glass milk bottle, "either way it was a lazy wind," she said, pouring a drop into the bottom of each cup.

Dad nodded his head, "it certainly was."

"What's a lazy wind?" I asked, looking up from my book as Mum poured out the tea.

## Wendy Hamilton

"A wind that is too lazy to go around you so it cuts right through," said Dad. "I remember when Steve and I were building the city's clock tower, feeling so cold I thought I would die."

A small splattering of rain bounced on the metal roof in a loud staccato of pings.

"We need the toilet closer," said Mum, looking up, "I'm sick of trailing across to the other paddock, especially in the rain."

"Hmm," said Dad, taking the cup Mum handed him. He wore his thinking face.

"And it's spooky going under all those trees in the dark," chipped in Rubella.

"Yeah, I'm always scared a possum might jump on me," I said, remembering the time a friend's pet possum jumped on Antoinette's head.

"What do you mean by hmm, Harold?"

"I'm sick of having to empty the toilet bucket every day," said Dad, taking a sip of tea. He swallowed. "I'm thinking to dig a really deep hole and have everything drop directly into it."

"What if we fall into it?" said Rubella, alarmed.

"You won't fall into it, it won't look any different," Dad reassured her, "it will still look like a toilet seat on a wooden box, you won't see the hole underneath when the seat is down." He took another sip of tea.

"Oh Harold, that sounds like a lot of work," said Mum, as the noise on the roof increased, "I was hoping we could shift it sometime soon."

## Little House in the Bush

"It will save me work in the long-run," said Dad. He drained his cup and set it down on the saucer with a click. "I will go and dig the hole now."

"But it's raining, you'll get wet," objected Mum.

"I'll be alright," said Dad, pulling his black oilskin coat on and thrusting his feet into gumboots. He picked up his spade and twisted the doorknob. As soon as the latch yielded, the door flew open and the wind rushed about the room, rattling and swinging anything that was not rigid. Dad leaned into the gale as he stepped outside, and pulled the door shut behind him. Instantly everything stopped rattling and swinging. He was away for a long time. At last the door opened again and Dad blew into the room.

"I need everyone to help shift the toilet," he said, forcing the door shut.

"Do I have to come," said Antoinette, untwisting a length of thread from a cotton reel and biting it off. She squinted as she threaded a needle. "I need to finish my sewing project. Mrs. Hartley said our sewing assignments have to be in by the end of next week."

"We need everyone," said Dad, leaning his spade against the wall, "it won't take long."

Antoinette threw down the calico nighty she was making and pouted. Her lips looked unnaturally large and red.

"What's that on your lips?" said Mum, eyeballing her.

Antoinette whisked the pout off her face and her lips

popped back into place.

"Lipstick," she said proudly, "I bought it with my pocket money."

"You're too young to be wearing lipstick," said Mum, frowning.

"Meagan wears lipstick to school," said Antoinette, her lips sticking out again. "Why can't I?"

"You can play with it at home but you're not wearing it to school," said Mum, compromising.

"Hurry up get your raincoats on," said Dad, "we need to get this done before we lose the daylight."

We gathered by the side of the door where the raincoats hung on four-inch nails. A mound of gumboots lay higgledy-piggledy underneath.

"I can't find one of my gumboots," said Rubella, hauling her coat off the rack and fossicking through the mound.

"None of the girls at school have to shift toilets," said Antoinette, pulling on a bright yellow coat.

"I'm getting very tired of hearing what the girls at school do or don't do," said Mum, slipping her feet into rubber gumboots.

I bent my head and hid a smile in the hood of my raincoat, as I pulled on my boots. It was nice to hear someone say aloud what we all thought.

"Hurry up don't dillydally," said Dad, handing Rubella her missing gumboot. He opened the door and we trooped out into the howling wind and the stinging rain. Rubella was the last out. She hopped on one foot

## Little House in the Bush

for a few steps as she pulled on her other boot. Once she was out, Dad pulled the door closed and it shut with a bang.

"Ooh, it's freezing out here," I moaned, shivering as water ran down my raincoat and dripped into the wide mouth of my boots.

"The sooner we get the outhouse shifted, the sooner we can go back inside," said Dad, striding to the front of the straggling line.

We followed him down the slope to the track that ended in the quarry. As we rounded the puriri tree, the full force of the wind whistling up the long valley, hit us. Our feet scarcely touched the ground as it blew us through the gate and over to the outhouse.

"I'm going to tip the shed on its back," yelled Dad, opening the door of the tall thin building with difficulty. He took out the bucket and toilet seat and put them in the lea of the wind, behind the wide trunk of a rotund tree. "I want you to catch it on the count of three."

We nodded as he shut the door and flipped the wire latch shut.

"One, two, three," he shouted.

We caught it clumsily. Mum, Rubella, and Antoinette held one side while Dad and I held the other.

"Let's go," Dad said, moving forward.

We followed him as best we could, like a set of pallbearers carrying a corrugated-iron coffin. My hands smarted and the outhouse joggled unpleasantly against my elbow as we shuffled out of step. Walking (like riding

## Wendy Hamilton

a bike) was much harder now the wind was against us. Our feet turned to lead as we fought to move forward. Dad twisted his head without breaking his stride.

"Keep going, it will get easier once we get around the puriri tree," he shouted encouragingly.

We battled onward, creeping closer to our goal slowly. The smarting in my hand turned to a dull ache as my burden slipped lower and lower into my fingers. Just when I thought I might drop it, the wind eased as we rounded the puriri tree and Dad shouted, "OK everyone, rest. Put her down gently."

In our eagerness to obey, we did not manage to lower it as gently as Dad wished. Nevertheless, we didn't actually drop the beastly thing. I opened and shut my red hands and blew on my cold fingers, until Dad gave the command to shoulder our burden again.

"Head towards the hole," said Dad. He pointed to the top of the hill where his spade stood like a golf flag in a mound of loose orange dirt, beside a pile of big rocks.

We staggered onwards and upwards until we reached our goal.

"Rubella and Anne, you can let go, Wendy and Antoinette, put your end down SLOWLY," said Dad holding onto the roof at the opposite end.

Mum and Rubella (delighted) obeyed instantly. Meanwhile, Antionette and I carefully lowered the bottom of the outhouse to the ground as Dad pushed his end skyward.

## Little House in the Bush

"It's not over the hole," said Rubella, as she looked down into the deep pit.

"It will be soon," said Dad, taking hold of the sides and rocking the building towards its final destination, in small increments.

A big gust of wind blew and the shed almost toppled out of Dad's grasp.

"Oh Harold," said Mum alarmed, "I don't want to be sitting in there and have it blow over!"

"It will be alright, I'll anchor it down," said Dad settling it into position, "Come here kids," he called, "hold this for a minute."

We scuttled over and held the outhouse upright, while Dad stacked the pile of rocks around the base of the building, and shovelled loose dirt into the cracks between them.

"There, that will do," he said at last, wiping the dirt off the blade of his spade with a fistful of long grass.

We let go cautiously. Another big gust blasted against us, pushing Rubella backwards. All eyes locked on the small building; it shook slightly but stayed upright.

"That's not going anywhere in a hurry," smiled Dad, slapping the wall with his hand in a friendly manner. "You can all go inside while I finish here," he said generously, as he strode off to collect the toilet seat and empty the stinking bucket.

The sun was sinking rapidly and inside the garage it was almost dark when we stumbled through the door. Mum lit a tilly lamp and sat it on the bench and

## Wendy Hamilton

I went about the room lighting a multitude of candles; each one jammed into the neck of a milk bottle. Very soon a savoury smell filled the room as Mum cooked up a pan of rice risotto. Rubella and I started a game of knucklebones, while Antoinette picked up her interrupted sewing.

"Wait until Dad comes in and lights the big lamp," said Mum, turning around and looking at Antoinette, "you don't want to ruin your eyes by sewing in poor light."

Antoinette sighed, put down her school project and rattled about in her sewing bag for her new lipstick. When she found it, she held it up to a candle to admire its gold case.

"Oh, that's pretty," I said admiringly.

"It's called Royal Red," said Antoinette going all British. She twisted the end so the new and sharply moulded tip protruded, before pouting and squinting into the cracked and spotty surface of a mirror on the wall. I shivered inwardly at her daring as she coloured in her lips. Although Antoinette was eighteen months younger than me and shorter, she managed to pass for older. Moreover, she was not intimidated by the outward trappings of womanhood as I was. She could not wait to strut around in makeup, stockings, and high heels. The divide between us was so great on this issue, I wondered if perhaps she really was a princess born to jewels and the soft life, while I was born to pit toilets and Taranaki gates.

## Little House in the Bush

Dad came in.

"You were quick," said Mum, "I thought it would take you longer to empty the bucket that that."

"Oh, it was easy," said Dad, taking down the big pressure lamp and lighting the wick under the mantle, "like I said, digging a deep hole will save me time in the long run." He pumped the small handle in the lamp's base as if he were pumping up a bike tire. "I just tipped everything down the toilet and washed the bucket." He stopped pumping and turned a small lever. There was a pop as the mantle sprang into life and light flooded the room.

"That's good," said Mum, stirring the pan to stop the rice from sticking to the bottom.

Antoinette put the top back on her lipstick, dropped it in her sewing bag, and picked up her school project. There was no doubt about it, Antoinette was talented at sewing. The snowy white nighty was lovely. It had puffed sleeves and was embroidered around the high neck with pink bullion roses, flanked with small green leaves. The whole thing was painstakingly stitched together by hand and a marvellous example of heirloom sewing.

"Dinner," said Mum putting five plates on the table and dishing up.

We put away our activities and sat down at the table. The lamp drew a circle of yellow light around us and I ate my dinner happily. I loved this simple basic way of life. By the bench a large kettle simmered on the stove, so we would have hot water for washing the dishes when we were finished.

Later that evening, Mum sat in bed and knitted, while Dad read, and Rubella and I played cards. Antoinette, meanwhile, sewed diligently. Suddenly she snipped the last thread off, stuck the needle in a pincushion and shook out her nighty.

"There, I'm finished," she said, holding it up for us to look at. "Oh Antoinette, that is wonderful," raved Mum, pausing in her knitting.

Dad looked up from his book, "very good indeed."

"I wish it was mine," said Rubella, putting a seven of diamonds on the pile of cards between us.

"You will get an A-plus for sure," I said, putting an ace on top.

Antoinette smiled at our praise. "It was hard work, but now that it is finished it was worth it."

Rubella reached out to finger the ruffle around the hem.

"Don't touch it!" said Antoinette, whipping it out of her grasp, "I don't want it dirty."

"My hands are not dirty," said Rubella huffily, "they are perfectly clean."

"You never know," said Antoinette, folding her nighty carefully and laying it tenderly in her sewing bag, "fingers have oil in them. If you want to touch it you have to put a white glove on first, the way they do at quilt shows."

"I don't have a white glove," said Rubella.

# Little House in the Bush

*We carried the outhouse like pallbearers*

## Wendy Hamilton

"Then I guess you won't be touching it," said the family princess, looking down her nose.

"I didn't want to touch your crumby old nighty anyway," said Rubella, turning back to her cards.

"Well Aim gooing to bed," said Antoinette, through Royal Red lips as she picked up her bag and rose from her chair.

"Make sure you wipe that lipstick off," said Mum, "I don't want it on the sheets, makeup is really hard to get off."

Antoinette (ignoring Mum's comment with regal disdain) picked up a candle and opened the door. The wind, as if it were at a party, blew out the flame with a single huff.

"Take the hurricane lantern," said Dad, pointing to the tilly lamp on the bench.

Antoinette swapped the candle for the lamp and turned the doorknob cautiously. The wind threw the door open as it rushed past her and swirled about the room, its icy fingers scattered my pile of cards, while breezy tendrils, sneaked around the edge of the lantern's glass, causing the flame to flicker violently. Antoinette hurriedly slammed the door shut and the flame straightened into a trembling tongue.

"Next time, use your body and your other hand to shelter the lantern," said Dad.

Antoinette poked her arm through the handles of her sewing bag, and slid it down into the crook of her elbow, before opening the door again. As the wind rushed

## Little House in the Bush

in, she twisted quickly and the flame stopped leaping about. "Can someone shut the door for me?" she asked, backing out of the room, "my hands are full."

I ran over and shut the door behind her. None of us expected to see her until morning, so it was a surprise when a few minutes later the door burst open, and Antoinette rushed in sobbing.

"What's happened?" said Dad leaping up and grabbing the iron frying pan like a weapon. "Did you see a possum shooter?"

"Nooo, nothing like that," bawled Antoinette. "It's my nighty."

"What about your nighty?" said Mum, alarmed by Antoinette's distress.

"It's gone!"

"What do you mean it's gone?" said Mum mystified, "where's it gone."

"Down the toilet!" wailed Antoinette.

Rubella and I started giggling.

"Don't laugh, it's not funny," said Antoinette, glaring at us and stamping her foot.

"That's right," said Mum, giving us the LOOK. "How did it happen?"

"The lantern blew out just as I got to the outhouse, and I needed both hands to get the door shut, so I put my sewing bag on the toilet seat. But SOMEONE," Antoinette glared accusingly at each one of us, "SOMEONE had left the lid up!"

"Let's go and get it," said Dad, pulling on rubber

gloves. He handed Antoinette a flashlight and a bucket, before picking up the long-handled hoe leaning next to his spade.

They were gone for ages but eventually the door opened and they blew in.

"Did you get it?" asked Mum, pausing in her knitting.

"Yup," said Dad, "it took a while but eventually I managed to hook it out."

"Pooh it stinks," said Rubella, holding her nose.

"Do you think the brown stains will come out, Mum?" sniffed Antoinette sadly.

"Soak it in Nappysan," said Mum, "that gets most stains out."

"What about your lipstick," I asked, "did you manage to fish that out too?"

"No," said Antoinette giggling suddenly, "I told Dad not to bother." Without a trace of Britain in her accent she added, "I'm not keen on that lipstick anymore."

**Little House in the Bush**

# Substitute Horses

My friend Jane was horse crazy. I never understood her obsession until she took me riding one day. I came home with only one thing on my mind.

"Mum, can I have a horse?" I shouted, staggering through the door with a stack of borrowed books.

"If you pay for it yourself," agreed Mum, secure in the knowledge my pocket money was two dollars a week. "And take those filthy jeans off before you sit on the couch. You are not in the bush now."

"Can we live at Mount Tiger all the time?" I said, imagining myself riding every day and lounging about in dirty jeans.

"Don't be silly," said Mum dismissively, "this is a lovely house and a very good area." She flicked back to my jeans, "and don't leave them lying on the floor, I'm not your maid, put them in the dirty-washing basket."

## Wendy Hamilton

I sighed and went to my room to change. Sometimes it was hard living with a house-proud mother. The books lay tantalizingly on my bed as I hauled off my trousers and pulled on a clean pair. 'Horse and Pony, Caring for Your Horse, Horse Etiquette, The Complete Horse and Pony'. I poured over the pictures of thoroughbreds and show jumpers. The horse's coats were shiny and the riders nattily dressed in jodhpurs and jackets, boots, and black velvet hats. Even the terminology within the pages oozed magic; saddle, bridle, snaffle bit, curry comb, saddle soap, three-day events. I lapped it up and faithfully saved my pocket money week after week.

"It is going to be a long time before I have enough for a horse," I said glumly to Antoinette one day.

"Your birthday's coming up soon," she reminded me, "and I know what Mum has bought you."

"Have you been in Mum's closet again?" I asked perking up. Antoinette's skills at sniffing out presents were legendary in the family. Thanks to Antoinette, we seldom had any surprises on Christmas morning.

"Yup," said Antoinette, wallowing in the glory associated with a rare and valuable skill.

"What?"

"A riding hat."

"Really."

"Yup, it's black velvet with a bow at the back and inside its purple."

For Mum's sake I pretended to be surprised when I unwrapped it on my birthday a few weeks later. It was

## Little House in the Bush

every bit as beautiful as Antoinette's description.

What even Antoinette had not seen coming, however, was an unexpected gift from an old man. I eyed the crop dubiously. Like most of the stock Mr. Core sold from his back shed, it was a feat of homemade ingenuity; a crude tongue of leather rammed into the end of a length of polythene pipe.

"It was very kind of Mr. Mc Core," I said pretending to look grateful. "I'm sure it would work just as well as a real one," I added, trying to find something nice to say.

"Don't forget to thank him and Grandma," said Mum.

"Of course not," I said, fingering Grandma's twenty-dollar note happily. I was glad Grandma had got over making us shell mice and pet rocks for birthdays and Christmas. Instead, she sent money which was always welcome, especially as (unlike Nana who rigidly sent two dollars) she kept abreast of inflation by increasing the amount as we grew. But even with this and regular lawn mowing jobs, I still had a long way to go before I got a horse. I had to make do with a humped mound at Mount Tiger. One day I was sitting astride it, pretending I was show jumping, when I had a brainwave. I went in search of Antoinette to tell her my idea. I found her and Rubella in the middle of our herd of cattle. The boys (who had become very tame) were sitting in the sun chewing their cuds contentedly, while Antoinette and Rubella read comics as they lounged over Poopsy.

# Wendy Hamilton

*Poopsy got rideable*

## Little House in the Bush

"Hey why don't we try riding Poopsy," I said walking over to them.

"I've never heard of anyone riding a cow," said Rubella, looking up from her comic.

"I saw men riding bulls when Meagan's father took her and me to see a rodeo, but it didn't look very safe," said Antoinette in an English accent.

"They are not cows or bulls," I said triumphantly, with the air of one who has just won an argument. "While I'm waiting for a real horse, we can practice by riding the boys."

"I suppose we could try," said Antoinette dropping into her normal voice, and scratching behind Poopsy's ear. Unaware of our plans for him, he flicked a fly lazily with his tail, swallowed his cud, and belched up another mouthful.

The herd, disturbed by my movement, started to get up. Antoinette and Rubella tumbled off as Poopsy rolled onto his knees and hoisted his back legs erect. When his front legs were also standing, I put my hands on his back and said, "give me a leg up, Antoinette."

She took my bent knee in her hand and boosted me onto Poopsy's back; my legs hung on one side and my arms on the other. Startled by this indignity, he ran a few steps forward before I slid off him.

"That's not riding," said Rubella critically.

"No, but it's a start," I said.

"I want to give it a go," said Antoinette forgetting she was a princess. "Give me a leg up."

## Wendy Hamilton

I hoisted her up and she lay across Poopsy for two minutes, before he took off and she slid to the ground. "Let's try again," she said brushing the mud off the seat of her pants.

"Do you want a go, Rubella?" I asked.

"Nah, I can't be bothered," said Rubella, picking up the fallen comics and wandering back to the shack.

"Give me another leg up, Wend," said Antoinette, as Poopsy dropped his head and started pulling grass with his tongue.

It took several weeks, but at last Poopsy and a few others got rideable. They were not as good as a horse but they were better than a grassy mound. Mostly Dad was tolerant and amused at our oxen training antics. Although occasionally our agendas clashed.

"Get off that beast before you run the beef off him," yelled Dad, as I galloped up a steep fence line astride Poopsy.

In truth, I wanted to do as I was told but it was too difficult. I was jammed at the edge of a stampeding herd between a barbed wire fence and another bullock.

"I think," I said weakly, as I slipped off safely at the top of the hill, "we need some method of steering and stopping them." But alas, it was never to be because Dad decided it was time for them to go.

"If we don't sell them now for another farmer to finish them off, we'll be selling them direct to the meatworks," said Dad, effectively silencing our protests.

And so, it was with great sadness, we loaded our

## Little House in the Bush

pets onto a cattle truck and waved goodbye. Almost immediately Dad bought another herd of weaners. We never tried to ride them as they got bigger, however, because by that time I had saved enough money for a real horse.

**Wendy Hamilton**

# A Beaut Bargain

I Lay stretched along the window-seat in the living room in town, reading a book. The story was an enthralling tale of an English girl (they were always English) who knew nothing about horses but passionately wanted one. (I immediately identified with her.) The beginning of the book told how Jillian bought an unsuitable horse at an auction by accident. The middle chapters were given over to the trials and tribulations of a complete beginner struggling with a wild racehorse, until a dashing young man down the road took a hand in the situation. It ended with Jillian and Brown Bullet winning a huge British horse show and being selected for the Olympic team. It was totally believable. I read the last sentence of the novel and shut the book softly.

"That was so beautiful," I said.

"Can I read it?" said Rubella. She was lounging on

## Little House in the Bush

her stomach on the floor. In front of her was a bumper edition of Word Puzzles.

"Sure," I said, sliding it across the carpet to her.

"Thanks," she said, as it hit her side. "What's a seven-letter word for bent?"

"Buckled," I said.

"Hmm, it might be." She took a pen out of her pencil case and wrote B.U. in the first two boxes of the crossword before pausing. "Do you spell buckled with two Cs or a C and a K?"

"I think it's two Ks," I said uncertainly.

Rubella nodded and wrote K.K.L.E.D in the rest of the boxes.

I picked up the newspaper and shook it open to the LIVESTOCK column in the classified ads. Maybe I might spot a bargain like the girl in the book, I thought. I had a lot of confidence in my ability to pick up a bargain, like the antique Hornby clockwork train set I got for five dollars at a garage sale. I ran my finger down the column, but everything was far more expensive than I expected. My hundred dollars looked less and less the more I read. I was almost in despair when my finger stopped on the last line. I grabbed a pen out of Rubella's pencil case and circled the advertisement.

"Mum!" I shouted, throwing the pen back, and running into the kitchen. "There's a horse for sale and they only want a hundred dollars!" I yelled, thrusting the paper at her.

Mum stopped wiping the oven, put her cloth down,

and took the paper from me.

"Mare, 14-hand $100 ono Ph 437 886."

"Please, could you ring, Mum, please, please, please?"

"Ono, or near offer," interpreted Mum, getting excited about a spot of wheeling and dealing, "I wonder if they would take eighty dollars?

Still clutching the paper, she walked into the square hallway and over to the wrought iron telephone table. The phone (a chunky box with a bulky receiver on a twisty cord) squatted on the glass tabletop. I followed her and sat on the adjoining padded seat as she put her finger in the fourth hole in the dial.

"Four," she said aloud, pushing the disk around. She took her finger out and there was a whirring sound as it revolved back to home-base.

"Three… Seven…Eight…"

As she dialled, I stared at the split staircase opposite, noticing without surprise, how one side descended to the basement and the other ascended to the bedrooms.

"Hello?" a woman answered.

"Hello, do you have a horse for sale?" asked Mum.

"Yes."

"Could you tell me a bit about it?"

With my finger I absently traced the twists in the white table leg as I honed in on the conversation. I gleaned from Mum's responses that the pony was eighteen-years-old, very quiet, and perfect for a beginner.

"She said we can go around and look at her, now,"

## Little House in the Bush

said Mum, putting down the phone.

"Yahoo," I shouted, leaping up.

"What's going on?" said Antoinette coming out of her bedroom and sliding down the wrought iron bannisters.

"I might be buying a horse," I said dancing around on the spot.

"When?"

"Now maybe. Do we have to go far?" I said, jiggling up and down in excitement.

"No, she's in Manu," said Mum, picking up her bag and taking the car keys from the junk drawer. "Everyone, get in the car," she called, walking down the staircase and opening the basement door. I ran after her and into the small room in the corner of the garage.

"Wait until I get my piggy bank and riding hat," I called, picking the china pig off the shelf and grabbing the hat off my bed. I looked at the crop sitting on my dressing table, hesitated, and decided against it. Mum had the garage door up and the car started by the time I tumbled into the backseat. Rubella sat in the front because she got there first. Of Antoinette there was no sign.

"Where's Antoinette?" said Mum.

"She went back to get her pink handbag," said Rubella.

Mum honked the horn and backed out. "Last one out, shuts the garage door," said Mum out the window as Antoinette rushed into the garage, slamming the basement door behind her.

Antoinette jumped up, grabbed the rope hanging off the handle of the big door and pulled it hard, skipping out of the way as it whooshed down and banged shut.

"Off we go," said Mum, letting out the clutch once Antoinette was safely in. The car whined as it backed up the long right-of-way and into the traffic.

Manu was an expensive area on the edge of town. Big houses sat on small acreages. Mum drove slowly along the manicured road as we all looked intently at the numbers on the letterboxes.

"There's 184," Rubella shouted, pointing to a tidy gateway.

Mum swung into the driveway in front of a two-storied house with dormer windows. "This property must be worth a packet," she murmured, as she stopped the car.

The door of the house opened and a woman wearing a long pearl necklace and carrying a bridle stepped out.

"Hello, you must be the ones who have come to try out the horse," she said, walking towards us.

"Yes," said Mum, slamming the door of the car shut and moving forward to meet her. "I'm Anne and this is my daughter Wendy. She's the one interested in the horse."

"I'm Joan Davidson," said the woman, smiling at Mum, "come this way." She led the way down the side of the house to a tidy paddock behind. "It's my daughter, Sally's, pony," said Mrs. Davidson, opening the farm

## Little House in the Bush

gate. "She has another horse now and we are running short on grazing, that is why we are selling Beauty."

I gave a little skip at the name and looked eagerly at the pony grazing between a ring of low jumps. She was bay with a blaze running down her nose, and white socks. I was dizzy with joy. After months of mowing lawns and drooling over photographs, I was finally on the brink of owning a horse. It wasn't until we got closer that fantasy and reality parted company. The book horses had sleek coats that shone like polished brass. Beauty, by contrast, had a thick woolly coat, flecked with grey. Moreover, there were deep hollows above her eyes and I hadn't noticed any of the book specimens having those. In addition, Beauty's muzzle was quite different. The book horses had firm little black muzzles, while hers was pink and covered in big black spots. Her top lip twitched above her hairy lower lip that sagged open like a heavy school bag with a broken zipper.

"Is he a boy?" asked Rubella, looking underneath at the pendulous udder.

"No, she has had eighteen foals," said Mrs. Davidson explaining the mysterious appendage.

I thought this added to Beauty's mystique. I did not stop to wonder how she managed to have a foal every year of her life, including the year she was a foal herself. I stroked her as Mrs. Davidson pulled a bridle over Beauty's head, slipping the bit over her long teeth.

"There, now you can try her," said Mrs. Davidson, handing the reins to me. "Oh dear, I've forgotten the

## Wendy Hamilton

saddle," she said, fluttering her hands uncertainly. "I wish my daughter was here, I don't know much about horses."

"Don't worry, I don't need a saddle," I said, thinking of my rides on Poopsy, "I'm used to riding bareback."

"You must be a good rider," said Mrs. Davidson impressed.

"I wouldn't say that," I said, handing my piggybank to Mum and standing on one leg.

Antoinette boosted me onto Beauty's back. She felt warm and soft. Moreover, she never moved a hoof as I fumbled around with the reigns trying to work out how to hold them the way the books showed. That which looked so easy on the page, eluded me in reality. In the end, I let them dangle limply, and held onto a fistful of mane instead. At length, sitting still became a little tame so I flapped my legs and Beauty ambled forward, jerking her head up whenever her left front leg touched the ground.

"She got kicked in the knee at pony club the other day and now she is limping," said Joan, explaining the nodding.

Beauty and I hobbled around the circumference of the paddock and back to the little group watching us. As we crept to a halt, I leaned forward and put my arms around her neck. I was thirteen and in love for the first time.

"I want her," I said passionately.

Mum felt the lump on Beauty's left knee with the

## Little House in the Bush

professional touch of someone who knows how to drive a bargain.

"Would you take eighty dollars for her, Joan?" she asked in an undecided tone, looking at the knee.

Mrs. Davidson looked at the knee and paddock. The grass was as short as the lawn on a golfing green.

"If you take her straight away," she nodded.

"Tomorrow is Saturday," I said, jumping up and down.

"We could come for her early tomorrow morning," agreed Mum, handing my piggy bank back to me.

I shook out Grandma's twenty-dollar-note, Nana's two-dollar note, and one-hundred-and-eighteen fifty-cent coins, and counted them slowly into Mrs. Davidson's hands. With each coin my spirit soared higher and higher. This was an even better score than my Hornby train set. Beauty was a beaut bargain!

**Wendy Hamilton**

# On the Brink of Horse Ownership

We did not go out to Mount Tiger as usual, the Friday evening I bought Beauty. That night stretched out longer than Christmas Eve and the hours ticked by with agonizing slowness as I tossed and turned. Early the next morning (despite little sleep) I bounced out of bed and pulled on my clothes hastily. I made the porridge (my regular chore) and slapped spoons and bowls on the table.

Dad came down the stairs and into the kitchen. "You're up early," he smiled, opening the back door and slipping *[6]jandals on his feet. "I wonder what could be so exciting about today that you are getting your jobs done so quickly?" he teased.

---

6   New Zealand term for thongs or flip-flops.

## Little House in the Bush

"Nothing at all, it's just an ordinary day," I joked back.

He laughed and went off to get the milk from the bottom of the letterbox as he did every morning. I heard his footsteps fading as he jogged down the path, along the driveway, over a small bridge and up the long right-of-way to the cluster of letterboxes at the end.

"Why are you setting the table, that's Rubella's job?" asked Antoinette, wandering in as I put plates under the bowls and knives next to the spoons.

"You know Rubella, she will try to slow things down because she knows I want to get going," I said, with the conviction born from experience.

"Yeah, you're right," said Antoinette, lifting the toaster out of the cupboard and popping slices of bread in the slots, "she's always looking for an opportunity to annoy us and get us into trouble with Mum."

"I'm not going to take the bait today," I said, putting jars of homemade Lemon-Honey and tomato jam on the table.

"That will be tricky," said Antoinette, "you know what Dad says about her, 'have crisis will perform.'"

"This isn't a crisis," I said, "it's something wonderful."

"Doesn't make any difference, Rubella doesn't like to share the spotlight."

"Yeah, I know, that is exactly why I'm doing her job; it's one less thing she can slow up."

I heard the sound of jogging outside the window and

shortly after, the backdoor swung open and Dad walked in carrying six bottles of milk. As he put the wire milk basket on the bench, Mum arrived and plugged in the electric jug.

"You do know, we can't go too early, don't you?" she said, looking at me with raised eyebrows, "it would be rude to get Mrs. Davidson out of bed."

"I suppose," I agreed reluctantly, "but Mrs. Davidson does want Beauty out of the paddock as soon as possible," I reminded her.

"Hmm, she did seem overly anxious," agreed Mum, warming the teapot.

"And it's a long trek to Mount Tiger," I added. "How long will fifteen miles take us?" I asked, looking at Dad who was a mine of information on all kinds of things.

"A horse can walk thirty miles a day," said Dad.

"Then we should be at Mount Tiger by lunchtime," I said doing a little hop.

"I could give Joan a ring after breakfast and ask what time we can come," said Mum, spooning tea out of the tea caddy into the pot, and pouring in hot water.

"Yes please," I said, walking into the adjoining room. Mum followed me as I pulled a chair out from the grey formica table and sat down.

"Time to get up Rubella, breakfast," called Dad sitting opposite me.

Rubella slouched into the room still wearing her pyjamas. Her open bathrobe fell halfway down one shoulder and the floppy belt trailed along the floor

## Little House in the Bush

behind her like a mouse's tail. She shot me a sideways look from under her hooded eyelids.

"I don't feel well," she said, drooping her mouth pathetically. She made her eyes huge and stared at Mum as she came through the door.

"Oh dear," said Mum looking worried, as she put the teapot on the table. She felt Rubella's head with the back of her hand. "You don't feel hot," she said, relieved. "Where does it hurt, Pussycat?"

Under the veranda of Mum's hand, Rubella shot another hooded look at me and a secret smile lurked around the corners of her mouth.

"My stomach feels sore and I sort of ache all over," she whispered, opening her eyes wide again as Mum took away her hand.

"Perhaps you're getting a stomach bug," said Mum, "it might be wiser not to have anything to eat."

The delicious aroma of hot toast followed Antoinette into the room as she put the toast rack on the table, and slid into the padded bench between the table and the wall.

"It is not that sort of sore," said Rubella hastily, "I don't feel like porridge," she added, grimacing at the bowls of oatmeal. Her voice dropped back into a whisper, "but I think I could manage some toast if it was covered in thick butter and shop-bought jam."

"All right," said Mum, getting a jar of raspberry jam out of the cupboard.

"Shop-bought jam!" exclaimed Antoinette in a loud

healthy voice, "can I have some too?"

"No," said Mum, "you know we only have shop-bought jam on special occasions."

"Why can Rubella have some and not me?" said Antoinette indignantly.

"She's not feeling very well," said Mum, smoothing Rubella's hair.

Rubella smirked as she slid onto the bench beside Antoinette and took a piece of toast. She troweled on butter thickly and slowly spread shop-bought jam over top; all the while she gloated at Antoinette from the corners of her eyes.

"I'm not sure what to do now," said Mum uncertainly, "perhaps we could leave getting the horse until later this morning. Then I can see if Rubella gets better or worse."

"There's nothing wrong with her, she's just faking," I said.

"Are you a nurse, Miss-Know-All?" said Mum. Without waiting for a reply, she turned to Dad. While her back was turned, I snatched the opportunity to poke my tongue out at Rubella. "I'm not sure what to do?" she said biting her fingernail.

"You go, Anne," said Dad coming to my rescue, "she can stay here in bed. I'm planning to weed the garden today."

"That will work," said Mum brightening.

"I'm feeling a lot better all of a sudden," said Rubella her eyes popping back to their normal size. The idea of

# Little House in the Bush

being stuck in bed without an audience did not appeal to her. "I think I just needed something to eat."

"That's good, Pussycat," said Mum smiling.

The rest of the meal passed uneventfully. Once the dishes were done, and Mrs. Davidson confirmed it was not too early, Mum, Antoinette, Rubella, and I hurried into the car.

Finally, the moment had come, I was about to get the pony of my dreams.

**Wendy Hamilton**

# Not a Book Horse

Beauty was just as lovely as I remembered her. I walked up to her, uncoiled the rope I held and slipped it over her neck.

"Would you like to borrow my daughter's bridle until you get your own?" asked Mrs. Davidson kindly.

"Yes please," I said, recoiling the rope and taking the bridle she handed me, "thank you very much."

I looked at the tangle of leather straps and buckles in dismay. I knew the bit went in the mouth but the rest was a mystery. Like hand positions on the reigns, the diagrams in the books oversimplified the confusing reality.

"Here, let me help you," said Mrs. Davidson. "I'm not much good at this but I think it goes on this way."

After a few false starts we managed between us to get it on.

"I think it might be inside out," she said critically, as

## Little House in the Bush

we struggled to buckle the cheek strap.

"It looks alright to me," I said, getting it done at last, "does it matter if it is inside out?"

"Probably not," said Mrs. Davidson, her face clearing.

"Rubella and I'll follow behind in the car," said Mum.

"Do you want to come with me, Noo?" I asked Antoinette, calling her by her pet name.

"Yeah, that would be fun," she nodded without a trace of princess. "Do you want a leg up?"

The moment I had been dreaming of, had arrived at last. Once again, the books had oversimplified the reality. All the book horses fitted neatly on A4 pages. Beauty was tall compared to Poopsy, huge compared to the cat, and gigantic compared to a photograph. Although I did not want to admit it to myself, I was nervous of her.

"She has a sore leg," I said chickening out, "I think it would be better not to ride her."

"Very sensible," nodded Mum.

We said goodbye to Mrs. Davidson, and then with Antoinette at my side, and Beauty hobbling behind us, we walked out the gate, down the driveway, and along the footpath. Cars whizzed past us at an alarming rate, but Beauty (to my relief) ignored them. Mum and Rubella following in the car, crawled along on the other side of the road keeping us just insight. After a mile without mishap, my confidence started to rise and I was able to concentrate on another pressing matter.

"I don't think the name Beauty suits her," I said to Antoinette. "It's not that she isn't beautiful, because she certainly is, it just seems a very boring name."

"You could call her Trotwood," said Antoinette, who had just finished reading David Copperfield.

"Trotwood," I giggled, "that's a good name for a horse, but it's a boy's name."

"What about Trotter?" said Antoinette

"No, that makes me think of a pig."

For the next few miles, we walked along thinking up and rejecting names. Meanwhile, Beauty (two paces behind) kept up a rhythmical clip-clopping. By midday, we had settled on the name Wuzzel, but we were not much closer to our destination. In fact, we had not made it past the centre of town.

"I don't think Dad was right when he said horses can walk thirty miles in a day," I said. "It's lunchtime and we have only gone about three miles."

"At least she is following nicely," said Antoinette.

As the words left her mouth, the clip-clopping suddenly stopped, and the slack in the reigns tightened, yanking me backwards as I kept moving but Beauty did not. The invisible rubber band between horse and home had reached its limit. Once again, the books failed me. Not even 'Doctor Horseman' mentioned this annoying trait every rider contends with. I am speaking of the dawdling walk a horse moves away from home and the spanking trot (or faster) he returns.

## Little House in the Bush

"Why won't she move?" said Antoinette stopping.

"I dunno," I said, moving my shoulder in a slow circle.

"Pull her," suggested Antoinette.

"In a minute, I think my shoulder may be dislocated," I said, moving my arm up and down. When I knew it was not necessary to go to the hospital after all, I did as Antoinette said, and using two hands I leaned forward and pulled. Wuzzel responded by locking her legs, raising her head, and stiffening her neck.

"What now?" I said, brushing strands of hair off my sweaty red face.

"Try turning her around," said Antoinette, "perhaps that will get her started again."

It was a smart idea. As soon as we turned homeward, Wuzzel's head went down, her legs moved forward, and the reigns connecting us sagged. But as soon as I tried to circle back, she froze into a statue once more.

Mum, seeing our trouble, parked the car at the side of the road and came over.

"What's happening?" she said.

"Wuzzel won't move, at least she won't move any direction other than back the way we've come," I said in a wobbly voice.

"Try using this," said Rubella, handing me Mr. Mc Core's gift.

"Thanks," I said, "here Antoinette, take this and give Wuzzel a whack on the bottom while I pull her forward."

Antoinette was justifiably nervous of this suggestion. "What if she kicks?"

"I don't think she will, Mrs. Davidson said she never kicks."

Antoinette was not keen to test this theory and neither were Mum or Rubella.

"Here, you all pull while I whack her," I said, with the courage born of desperation.

But alas, even with Antoinette, Rubella, and Mum pulling one end, while my birthday present smacked the other end, Wuzzel's legs remained locked to the tarmac.

"This is a pickle," said Mum as we stood in a defeated huddle, "what on earth are we going to do?"

Wuzzle, unperturbed, dropped her head, closed her eyes, and tipped a back hoof onto tiptoe.

"I don't know," I said, close to tears.

Just when everything looked hopeless, a small miracle happened. Even the strongest rubber band can be broken by friendship. 'Horses are herd animals,' said the books and in that at least, they were right. In the distance, growing louder by the minute, came a faint clip-clopping. Wuzzel, hearing it, woke up, swung around, and whinnied loudly.

Once again, my shoulder experienced a wrench as the slack jerked out of the reigns I held. This time, however, Wuzzel was the one leading.

"Hang on," shouted Antoinette "don't let her go!"

"That's what I'm trying to do," I bawled back, skidding and slipping as I tried to slow Wuzzel's sudden

## Little House in the Bush

rush of speed.

"Perhaps that nice little girl with the horse would help us," said Mum squinting beyond the traffic lights. She ran back to the car and zoomed ahead.

By the time Wuzzel dragged us to the tall black horse, Antoinette and I were hot and very bothered. We bent over (our hands on our knees) and caught our breath as Wuzzel and Prince sniffed noses.

Mum, finishing her conversation with the rider on the horse, turned to us.

"This lovely little girl" (Mum's standard description for any female under twenty) "has said she will lead the way home."

"I don't think we can get all the way to Mount Tiger today," I said doubtfully. The morning's dose of reality had knocked fantasy off its perch. The idea of galloping fearlessly over smooth fields, barely breaking our stride as we cleared four-foot fences (horse and rider in total harmony) suddenly lacked credibility.

"I meant Kamo Road," said Mum.

"The section is too small for a horse, and Dad will have mown the lawn by now," I said, seeing many objections to the plan. "Besides, we don't have a gate; even if we tied Wuzzel up, she might get loose and run out into the traffic."

"Who's Wuzzel?" asked Mum, looking puzzled.

"Beauty. Wuzzel is her new name," I said proudly. "Don't you think it suits her better?"

"It certainly does," said Mum, looking at Wuzzel

who had gone back to sleep. "No, I was thinking of the empty paddock behind our stone wall," said Mum, returning to our former conversation.

"Mrs. Busk's paddock, the one by the gum trees?" I said fearfully. Once when I was small, Mrs. Busk caught me picking wildflowers in her field. The encounter was so traumatic I wet my pants.

"I'll go home and ask her," said Mum, like a fearless snake charmer, "I'm sure she won't mind."

"OK," I said, "just so long as I don't have to ask her."

"Of course not," said Mum. "I've told Janice," she pointed at 'the nice little girl,' "where to go, I'll head off now, see you soon."

We waved as she got into the car and zoomed away.

Janice turned Prince around and we clip-clopped all the way home.

Mum was right about Mrs. Busk she was more than happy to host Wuzzel for one night. As was Mr. Smith (the next day) whose farm lay halfway between our two properties. The fifteen-mile journey, Antoinette and I could have walked in a day, ended up taking three days because it was necessary to break it up into smaller distances for Wuzzel. Somewhere along the road, the vision of galloping effortlessly (rhythmically drumming hooves eating up the miles) died.

"I've gone off horse books," I said to Antoinette as we staggered into our paddock at Mount Tiger, "an ounce of practice is worth a pound of theory."

## Little House in the Bush

"What does that mean?" asked Antoinette as I took the bridle off Wuzzel.

"It means all those books are full of hogwash," I said, watching Wuzzel roll in the mud.

**Wendy Hamilton**

# A Bargain is Not Always a Bargain

"Saddles are so expensive," I said to my friend Maryanne. "Even second-hand saddles cost over a hundred dollars."

"How much have you got?"

"Only ten dollars. I had twenty, but I had to buy a bridle and that cost me ten."

Maryanne looked thoughtful. She was better to talk to than my horsey friend Jane, because Maryanne (unlike Jane) suffered similar financial restrictions.

"You could ask Mr. Mc Core if he has got a cheap saddle?"

"I suppose," I said doubtfully, thinking of my birthday crop. "Is it possible to make a saddle out of polythene pipe?"

## Little House in the Bush

"Quite impossible," Maryanne assured me. "In fact, I don't think it is possible to get a homemade saddle, they are too difficult to make."

There was a great deal of sense in her words. The lure of a bargain overcame my reluctance. Against my better judgment, I called Mr. Mc Core.

"A cheap saddle, aye. How cheap?" he wheezed down the phone.

"Ten dollars?" I said, feeling awkward.

"Ten dollars! That's not much, is it?"

"No," I agreed sadly, my heart plummeting.

"Well, I do have one I could let go for ten dollars," he said, "but only because it's you. I wouldn't sell it to anyone else for under a hundred dollars."

My heart lifted.

"Really?"

"Yes, really, but you have to say you'll definitely take it, because I've got others who want it."

"I do want it," I said, getting excited. "Oh, but I'd have to ask Mum if she would take me to your place to buy it."

"Don't worry your mother over a little detail like that," said Mr. Mc Core hastily, "if you have the money, I can deliver it to you when I come into town tomorrow."

"That would be wonderful," I said.

"Now do I have your word on it?" said Mr. Mc Core, "I don't want to turn down other buyers, bring it all the way into town, and then have you change your mind."

"No, I won't," I assured him.

### Wendy Hamilton

"Well, alright then, what time do you get home from school?"

"I'll be home by four," I said.

"Right, I'll be at your place by four tomorrow," said Mr. Mc Core. "Goodbye."

"Goodbye," I said, putting down the phone.

It was hard to stay focused at school the next day. My mind kept sliding back to the delicious expectation of a saddle. After several years, however, the last bell for the day sounded. I grabbed my bag and rushed home.

Mr. Mc Core arrived when he said he would and he delivered the saddle just as we agreed. Numbly I handed over my hard-earned cash and he left.

"Isn't it a bit big Wend?" said Rubella, as she eyed the leather monstrosity straddling Dad's sawhorse. Technically, it was a saddle. The leather leg flaps, however, looked like huge elephant ears while the top fanned out into a seat suitable for a bulldozer.

"It's a lovely saddle," I said smiling stiffly. I waited until Mr. Mc Core was out of earshot before drooping my mouth.

"Of course it is," I wailed, as his car backed out the driveway. "I had no idea saddles came this big!"

"It's awfully heavy," said Antoinette, lifting it up a few inches and letting it fall with a thump. "I think it is made to fit a carthorse."

"And a five-hundred-pound man," added Rubella.

"Why didn't you tell him you didn't want it?" asked Antoinette.

## Little House in the Bush

"Because I bought it before I saw it and I promised I wouldn't back out," I said holding up the stirrup leathers. "Look at this, the stirrups don't even match."

"You should never buy something sight unseen," said Antoinette wisely. "You never know what you might get. I once got a backscratcher in a Lucky Dip."

"I know that now," I said sourly. "How is my foot ever going to fit into this teeny little stirrup, it's made for a three-year-old? And the other one is so big my foot will slide right through."

"At least the five-hundred-pound man will be able to get one of his feet in a stirrup," giggled Antoinette.

"It is pretty funny," I said relaxing into laughter. "I suppose I can't expect much for ten dollars, at least I have a saddle. Wuzzel will be pleased, it will be more comfortable for her than my bony bottom."

I had had Wuzzel for a few weeks by now, and already she felt very much part of the family. She was a real character. Moreover, whatever she lacked in speed and looks, she certainly made up for in safety. We could ride her bareback, backward, or sideways. Bucking, biting, and bolting, just weren't in her nature. At the first opportunity, Antoinette and I approached her with the saddle. We carried it between us like a piano, resting every few yards until we got to her. Wuzzel's ears lost their relaxed floppy position when I (with great strength) hoisted the saddle onto her back. Instead, they flattened, her head shot up, and she let out a wheezy grunt. I leaned against her and rubbed my aching arms for a few minutes.

"Wow, that's heavy," I said to Antoinette. "I reckon it's heavier than me. It hardly seems fair to add my weight on top of it."

Antoinette nodded, too out of breath to speak. When we had all recovered sufficiently, I slid the girth under Wuzzel's belly, and buckled it up.

"I've never seen a girth like this before," said Antoinette critically, "do you think it is a real one?"

"Probably homemade," I said bitterly.

"What do you think it is, canvass or sacking?"

"I have no idea," I said tightening it. "I should have swapped the stirrups around," I added, "This one is too tiny to get my foot in, I'll need a leg up."

Antoinette boosted me up and Wuzzel's ears flattened again, her legs bowing with the extra weight. I put my right foot in the huge stirrup and the tip of my toes in the tiny left stirrup. Then I made a clicking sound with my tongue and kicked Wuzzel's sides gently. Obediently she staggered around the perimeter of the paddock. Every step the bulldozer seat scraped against the inside of my thighs painfully, and every third step I lost my toehold. What Wuzzel endured was beyond imagining.

"I don't know why people bother with saddles," I said to Antoinette when we got back to her, "they are so overrated. I'd rather ride bareback any day."

"I think Wuzzel would prefer it that way too," said Antoinette, helping me pull my ankle out of the big

## Little House in the Bush

stirrup.

"It's a good thing I didn't waste a lot of money on a saddle," I said sliding off and loosening the girth.

"Yeah," agreed Antoinette.

Together we cautiously pulled the saddle towards us. It fell into our arms like a cement truck. I released Wuzzel, and then Antoinette and I carried our burden back to the garage and dumped it next to the pile of gumboots.

"You were very quick," said Mum looking surprised, "I thought you would be gone for hours. How did the new saddle go?"

"A bargain is not always a bargain," I said, kicking the leather monstrosity languishing under the raincoats. "I'm glad I didn't buy my horse from Mr. Mc Core."

**Wendy Hamilton**

# Larry Lamb

Antoinette and I sat in her shed looking at her eraser collection spread over her bed.

"How many have you got now, Noo?" I asked.

"Almost a hundred and fifty," she said proudly. "Smell this one, it smells exactly like a strawberry."

I took the rubbery berry from her and sniffed. "Yeah, your right." I gave it back and picked up a rectangle with a transfer of a coconut stuck on the front. "These smell the best though," I said breathing in deeply.

"That's the only reason I keep getting them," said Antoinette, "they're boring but they smell so good I want to eat them."

I picked up a yellow car and sniffed.

"Don't bother smelling that one," said Antoinette, the interesting ones don't smell nice.

## Little House in the Bush

"I suppose it's hard to make a car-smell," I said, putting it down and picking up a red dog. "And dogs stink, nobody would want an eraser that smells of wet dog."

"No, and a strawberry smelling dog wouldn't be right."

I nodded. "What are you going to get Rubella for her birthday?" I said, changing the subject.

"I don't know," said Antoinette, wrinkling her brow as she fiddled absentmindedly with a blue monkey.

"I don't know either."

"I could get her some erasers," she said doubtfully.

"Nah, she's not into them."

"Yeah, you're right."

"What about watercolour paints," I said.

"Nah, you're the one that is into art, she's not interested. She is more into plants."

"We could get her a pot plant," I said brightening.

"Mum would get mad, she's sick of all the plants in Rubella's room, yesterday there was a big fuss because Rubella forgot to put a plate under her rubber-plant, and the pot has stained the carpet."

"You're right, that won't work either," I said deflating.

Antoinette, thinking hard, absentmindedly nibbled the edge of an eraser with an apple transfer. I squeezed a pink submarine and also thought hard. By nightfall, however, we were no closer to solving the problem.

At school the next day, my friend Angela was facing

a far worse problem. We mulled over her trouble as we sat on the slatted bench outside the science classroom.

"He's the cutest smartest lamb in the world" she wailed, taking an apple out of her lunch box.

"I'm sure he is," I said sympathetically, biting into my cheese and marmite sandwich, "pet lambs are always super cute."

"When he was little, his tail waggled like a helicopter blade whenever we fed him his bottle.

"I wish I could have a pet lamb," I said wistfully.

"He used to live in the kennel with the Alsatian," continued Angela. "Of course, he won't fit through the door anymore but he still thinks he's a dog. I can't bear to think of him lying between Brussel sprouts and potatoes, or worse still in my school sandwiches," she ended with a shudder, glancing at her lunch box.

Suddenly a light bulb lit up in my head. "I could buy him off you."

"It wouldn't make any difference whether he came to school in your lunch box or mine," sniffed Angela sadly.

"But we don't eat pet lambs."

"You don't!" she said, perking up before drooping again. "Then what would you want him for?" she asked suspiciously.

"My sisters' birthday. I've been racking my brains for weeks trying to work out what to get her. How much do you want for him?"

"I'd give him to you for free, but Dad will want the

## Little House in the Bush

twenty dollars the meat-works will give for him."

"My sister and I can find the money," I said, confident that Antoinette would want in on such a fantastic birthday present.

"That would be wonderful."

Angela and I beamed at each other. Both of our problems were solved with one simple solution. All our troubles were over; at least Angela's troubles were.

"Oh, he's so cute!" said Rubella when we went to pick him up after school the next day. "He's the best birthday present ever!"

We all stood around the enormous sheep admiringly.

"I knew you would like him," I said proudly, with the air of a magnificent provider.

"What's his name?" she asked Angela.

"Larry Lamb the fifth."

"Why the fifth?"

"Because he is the fifth lamb, we always call our lambs Larry."

It was obvious that Larry was not a lamb, but we overlooked the technicality.

"Larry's a good name for him," I said. I bent down and held out my hand for him to sniff in the vague hope it was the thing to do.

"Be careful when you bend down," cautioned Angela's mother, "he'll bunt you if you don't watch out."

"Oh dear," said Mum, stepping back anxiously as

Larry bounced towards us.

"Don't worry, he's only being friendly," said Angela's mother, "he just doesn't realize how big he is."

"Give him this," said Angela, handing Rubella a hard lump, "he loves guinea pig pellets. Hold your hand out flat."

"Here boy," Rubella said holding out her hand. Larry stretched his neck forward and nibbled the pellet. She gave a squeal of delight as his lips vibrated rapidly on her palm. "That tickles," she giggled.

"Feed him these while I tie a rope onto his collar," said Angela handing me a fistful of guinea pig pellets.

Antoinette, Rubella, and I took turns at giving Larry a pellet as Angela secured the rope. Then Mum opened the back hatch of the car, and Angela dragged Larry towards the open door. Larry, seeing the dog amble out of the house, changed direction and charged towards his old friend.

"Larry, not that way!" cried Angela, yanking at his collar.

I grabbed the rope and together we tried to pull him the way we wanted him to go, but it made little difference, Larry kept heading towards the dog.

"Help Antoinette," I yelled.

But even three of us were no match for Larry.

"Here, take these and I'll shut the dog in the house," said Angela's mother, shoving the bag of guinea pig pellets at Rubella.

## Little House in the Bush

Even with the dog removed it took all of us to drag Larry (Rubella leading the way with treats) into the back of the car.

"Well, at least we have the worst part over," said Mum naively, banging the door down and sliding into the driver's seat.

"He's the best birthday present ever," said Rubella, leaning over the top of the backseat and patting Larry's woolly head. Larry looked at her and licked his lips rapidly.

"He wants more guinea pig pellets," said Antoinette.

"Here boy," said Rubella, handing him one.

Mum put the car in gear and drove out the driveway and onto the gravel road. A horrible smell suddenly arose.

"I'm glad we put the tarpaulin down," said Mum wrinkling her nose. "You kids, make sure he stays in the back area."

"Yes," we chorused, and as long as the pellets lasted, we had no trouble. Just before Horror Hill, however, they ran out.

"What's all that commotion, what's happening?" said Mum as the car slewed around a hairpin corner. She glanced in the rear vision mirror. "I told you kids to keep that lamb in the back."

"We're trying to," I said, red in the face with exertion, "but he's hard to stop." I pulled his collar backwards, while Rubella pushed against his chest, and Antoinette tried to stop his legs coming up. Alas, it was futile; the enormous sheep forced his way over the back of the seat

"Stop him, stop him, he's climbing on top of me," yelled Rubella, her voice becoming muffled as she disappeared under him. She reappeared shortly after, as Larry bounced down into the ditch between us and the front seats.

"Don't let him eat your father's lemon tree or spill the Epsom salts," said Mum in alarm as his head popped between the front seats. In her agitation the car wobbled and swerved onto the other side of the road. Fortunately, there was nothing coming, everything was quiet.

Nothing was quiet inside the car, however.

"You two hold on to his collar," I said. Pulling Larry's head out of the gap, I leaned through the seats and pushed the lemon tree forward so the trunk fell against the dashboard and the leaves brushed the windscreen. Larry, now he was in the midst of us, settled down and the rest of the journey passed uneventfully. Nevertheless, it was a relief when we got to our gate. Mum stopped the car by the Pirrui tree and we got out as best we could without incurring more bruises than necessary.

"There you go boy," said Rubella, as Wuzzel and the cattle wandered over curiously. She untied the rope attached to Larry's collar, "go and meet your new friends."

Poopsy marched up and sniffed Larry, but Larry

## Little House in the Bush

showed little interest in him.

"Wendy, bring the bag of Epsom salts," said Mum. She picked up the lemon tree and carried it up the hill and into the bigger little house. Antoinette, Rubella, and I followed her, and Larry followed us... all the way inside.

"Get that lamb out of here!" said Mum, putting the tree on the table. "I'm starting to think this has been a mistake. Can we take him back?"

"Oh no," shouted Rubella, "he's my birthday present."

"We can't take him back, they won't have him," I said, as Antoinette and Rubella hustled Larry outside.

"What a pity," said Mum grimly.

"Where do you want the Epsom salts, Mum?" I asked changing the subject.

"Umm," said Mum hesitantly, "put them in the food box for the time being. Your father can decide where he wants them kept, once he has planted the lemon tree."

"He may use them all," I said, "how much does a lemon need?"

"I have no idea," said Mum. "You know me, I'm no gardener, I prune weeds and pull out plants. Hopefully there will be a little left. It's always good to have a bit of Epsom salts in the medicine cabinet."

"Why?" I asked, pulling a cardboard box out from underneath Mum and Dad's bed.

"They are very good for constipation," said Mum, as I put the salts next to a box of Weetabix, "they get things going again."

"Oh," I said, wishing I had not asked.

There was a commotion outside and Rubella squealed as Larry bounced about.

"You kids, don't let that lamb back in here," called Mum, "get into the car, Dad will be home for dinner soon. Hurry up, Wendy."

I pushed the box back under the bed and hurried outside. Mum slammed the door shut and locked it, then we raced down to the car with Larry running behind us.

"Look, he wants to come home with us," said Rubella, as Mum fought with Larry to get into the car, "can we take him home, he could eat the lawn."

"Over my dead body," said Mum fiercely. "This has been a huge mistake."

"Goodbye Larry," we called waving to him as we drove away, "we will see you on Friday night."

# Problems with Larry

The rain fell in a dense curtain as the car sloshed down the Mount Tiger driveway on Friday evening.

"I hope Larry made friends with Wuzzel and the boys," I said, wiping a circle in the steamy window and peering out. "I can't see him anywhere. I hope he is alright."

"Keep your feet on the newspaper," said Mum hearing rustling and shuffling, "I don't want your muddy boots getting on the carpet."

"Uh-huh," I nodded absently.

"He's probably under the trees somewhere," said Dad, parking the car a little way beyond the puriri tree.

"I can't wait for you to see him," said Rubella, "he's the best birthday present I ever had."

## Wendy Hamilton

"I might need to leave it until tomorrow," said Dad, looking at the hosing rain.

"Nobody is to leave the car empty-handed," said Mum, relieved there was no sight of Larry.

"I bags taking the cat," said Antoinette, lunging under Dad's seat and pulling Shnike out.

"That's not fair," I chimed in, "it's my turn."

"It was my birthday on Tuesday so I should be the one who takes him," pouted Rubella.

"Nobody is taking him," said Mum, handing Dad his gumboots, "he has legs he can get there himself."

"He might run off," I said anxiously.

"Not likely," said Dad, taking off his shoes awkwardly, "he'll probably beat you to the garage."

That shut us up because we knew it was true. Dad opened the car door and the rain blew in as he put his stockinged feet into his gumboots. Then he squelched around to the back and opened the hatch. Antoinette let Shnike out and the cat shot up the paddock as Dad predicted. I pulled the hood of my raincoat over my head and reluctantly stepped out into the rain.

"Take this," said Dad, passing me a tin of milk powder and a big bag of dried potato flakes. I took them and ran up the hill behind Antoinette, who carried a bumper pack of toilet rolls and her transistor radio.

"That's funny," puffed Antoinette as we got close to the garage, "the door is open."

"Dad," I shouted fearfully, as we both slowed to a halt, "someone has broken into the shed!"

## Little House in the Bush

Dad dropped the picnic basket, picked up a cast iron frying pan like a weapon, and came haring up the hill. He rushed past us and through the open door. There was a pause and Larry's head popped out the door.

"I take it this is Larry," said Dad pushing him outside.

"I thought that animal was a big mistake?" said Mum as we shooed Larry away and went inside, "now I know I was right."

"It appears Larry doesn't like getting wet," said Dad, "and what's more, he likes Weetabix and Epson salts," he added, holding the empty box and bag up.

"A big enormous mistake!" exclaimed Mum looking at all the smelly black marbles liberally scattered over the floor.

"It looks like Epson salts work on sheep the same way they do on humans," I said.

"You kids can clean them up," said Mum, giving Rubella a dustpan, Antoinette a brush, and me a bucket. "There is disinfectant and a scrubbing brush in the toilet, Wendy."

I ran up to the outhouse and grabbed them. When I got back, Dad was examining the door while Mum tried to mop up the worst of the wet patch on the floor.

"He's bunted this very hard," said Dad, looking at a huge dent in the aluminon door.

"I'm glad I brought more than one towel with me," said Mum, wringing water out of it into a bucket. She folded it into a thick wad threw it back on the floor.

# Wendy Hamilton

*Larry was sitting on Antoinette's bed*

## Little House in the Bush

"He's busted the catch," said Dad, straightening it again with a bang of his hammer.

"Can you fix it?" asked Mum treading on the towel.

"I think so. He's ripped the screws out, but I can screw them in again."

"Won't he bash it open again?" said Mum.

"Probably," sighed Dad. "I will have to put a metal latch and a padlock on the door to keep him out."

"Wait a minute, Wendy," Mum halted me on my way to the water drum on the bench. "Use rainwater. No point carrying more water than we have to.

"I trooped back outside to the corner of the shed and put my bucket underneath the drainpipe. In a short space of time it was half full.

"Did you see where Larry went?" said Rubella as I came in. She was holding the dustpan while Antoinette swept sheep droppings into it.

"No, I didn't," I said, kicking off my gumboots and hanging up my raincoat, before adding a dollop of disinfectant to the water. I dropped to my knees and followed behind my sisters, scrubbing lingering marks off the threadbare carpet.

"There, we are done," said Antoinette at last, straightening up. "Can I go now, Mum?"

"Yes," said Mum, wringing out the towel for the final time before chucking it in the dirty-washing bag.

"Thanks." Antoinette pulled on her gumboots and dashed into the rain. We did not expect to see her again until dinnertime, so it was a surprise when minutes later she burst into the room crying.

"What's the matter?" said Mum alarmed.

"I've found Larry," sobbed Antoinette.
"What's wrong with him?" I asked. "Is he sick?"
Antoinette shook her head. "No."
"Is he dead?" shouted Rubella.
"No, no," sobbed Antoinette, "he's alright. He's sitting on my bed."
"Has he bashed that door open too?" said Dad frowning, as he gave the final twist to the screw he was replacing.
"Uh-huh," nodded Antoinette. "And I think he has spent most of the week there, my sleeping bag is a mess."
"That animal has been a gigantic mistake," moaned Mum, "sleeping bags are so hard to wash, especially in this sort of weather!"
"That's not the worst," choked out Antoinette, "he's eaten my eraser collection!"
"All your one-hundred-and-fifty erasers?" I said shocked.
"Uh-huh," Antoinette nodded.
"Even the red dog and the pink submarine?"
"Uh-huh, he left a few of the boring ones but he ate the rest."
I could hardly believe it; the magnitude of the disaster was up there with an earthquake or a tsunami. "Even the blue monkey?"

## Little House in the Bush

"Most of him," said Antoinette, opening her hand to reveal Monkey's head.

"That is terrible," I said, feeling very sorry for my sister.

"The biggest problem," sniffed Antoinette unhappily, "is he is so cute I can't get mad at him."

"No," said Mum with thin lips and glaring eyes, "the biggest problem is not you can't get mad at him, the biggest problem is we can't eat him!"

**Wendy Hamilton**

# Goodbye to Town Life.

Dad was a patient God-fearing man. He was prepared to wait a long time for something he wanted. He quietly worked towards his goals while he waited for God to move. From a small boy he wanted to live by the bush. My mother, however, was a townie; born and bred. Moreover, she wanted to stay that way.

"You'll never get me living in the bush," she said often and with conviction. "Buying land on spec and a few weekends and holidays are one thing, but actually living out there, forget it!"

We may have yo-yoed between town and country indefinitely, if it were not for Mrs. Busk's trees. Mrs. Busks Blue Gums shaded our back yard, and more importantly, provided privacy. Their presence made

## Little House in the Bush

it possible to imagine our little patch of suburbia was in the country. Especially as our yard was bordered on two sides by fields, and so far down a long right-of-way, only the singing of the birds disturbed the peace. One day, however, the quiet was shattered by a hideous noise.

"That sounds like a chainsaw?" said Mum, alarmed, "I hope the neighbour's not cutting down the Weeping Willow."

"It doesn't sound like it's coming from the Wilson's place," I said as we rushed outside. "It sounds like it's coming from Mrs. Busk's field."

"It's the blue gums," shouted Rubella, pointing at the trees on the other side of the creek behind our stone wall. They sprang forth from the ground in a cluster of tall smooth trunks that dripped ribbons of bark and pungent eucalyptus leaves.

"Oh no, not the Blue Gums," said Mum, stomping over a small bridge, "it must be a mistake, Mrs. Busk would never allow it!"

I followed as far as the wire boundary fence but did not go any further. Ever since the traumatic wildflower episode years ago, I kept well away from Mrs. Busk. Mum, meanwhile, fearlessly climbed the fence and pushed her way through the long grass. The noise cut off as the workmen spotted my mother striding towards them her, lips a thin straight line. In the silence I heard Mrs. Busk's voice. It sounded like she was crying. I knew, however, that was impossible. I found it easier to imagine the Incredible Hulk crying than Mrs. Busk. While I waited, I picked sheep's wool off the twists of barbed wire absentmindedly. At length Mum came back with her arm around a little old lady.

"Come and have a cup of tea, Mrs. Busk," said Mum helping her over the fence.

I gave a start of surprise. Somehow in the last seven years, the towering ogre of my memory had shrunk into a frail elderly woman with birdlike bones, and grey hair twisted into a wispy French roll.

"When I donated the land to The Disability Society," sobbed Mrs. Busk tottering over the bridge, "it never crossed my mind they would cut down the trees. I grew them from seed and planted them myself."

"Perhaps you could call the Managing Director and get them to stop," suggested Mum, as they walked towards our back patio.

"I did," sniffed Mrs. Busk, wiping her eyes with a lace handkerchief, "but he said they have to come down for safety reasons."

All conversation was halted as the roar of chainsaws ripped through the air again. Once we were in the house, the noise dimmed as Mum shut the door and all the windows.

"What did they mean by safety reasons?" queried Mum, returning to the interrupted conversation.

"Apparently, gum trees are shallow-rooted and they could fall down," said Mrs. Busk forlornly. "I told them that was a load of rubbish but they won't listen."

## Little House in the Bush

"No, surely not!" exclaimed Mum, horrified at their insensitivity.

"I would never have given the land to the Disability Society if I had suspected they would do this," Mrs. Busk repeated sadly.

A crack like a pistol shot ran out, and a long trunk toppled over and hit the ground with a sickening thud. A tall thin line of houses suddenly appeared and suburbia peered down at us through the crack.

"Oh no," we all wailed, feeling as if a close friend had been murdered. It was horrid watching our privacy-protectors fall one by one in quick succession. By midafternoon, the sun blazed like an inferno into our yard and the eyes of a hundred houses gawped at us from the nearby hill.

"It's all over," said Mrs. Busk in a wobbly voice, "my trees are gone and there is nothing we can do about it."

Mum helped her back to her house, and for the rest of the afternoon the noisy racket continued as the men cut the trunks into firewood and chipped the small branches and leaves. When at last they were finished and gone, we thought the worst was over. As the light dimmed, however, another shock awaited us; lights shone out of hundreds of windows.

"I can't live like this," wailed Mum to Dad when he came home. Her needles flashed in and out rapidly as she poured her agitation into her knitting. "I don't even like going out to hang the washing on the line, I feel so exposed. Look at all those houses staring at us, I prefer Mount Tiger."

A gleam entered Dad's eye as he glimpsed the phycological moment to shift his town-bred wife into the country permanently.

"We could shift out there," he said cautiously, "it's very private in the bush."

"Good idea," said Mum without hesitating, her needles clicking furiously as she glanced out the ranch-slider.

"We would have to sell this house to finance the new one," said Dad, testing Mum's reaction.

"Fine," said Mum, finishing a row and turning her knitting around.

"You'd have to live with a pit toilet and no electricity, every day for six months," said Dad raising a questioning eyebrow.

"No problem," agreed Mum, starting another row.

"In the mountains, close to the bush, with the nearest neighbor a mile away?"

"Sounds idyllic," said Mum, shuddering at the hundred houses staring into the room.

"Among the wild goats and possums."

"Fabulous," said Mum, knitting so fast her needles almost smoked.

"I can cope with shifting provided you don't fall to bits emotionally," lectured Dad.

"I will love it," Mum assured him, finishing another row.

# Little House in the Bush

*"Oh no, not the blue gums!"*

## Wendy Hamilton

"Then on that condition I will consent," he conceded magnificently.

Antoinette, Rubella, and I leapt about the room hooting with joy. Even princess Antoinette wanted to live out in the bush with the cattle, Larry, and Wuzzel.

"The only thing I can't work out," said Mum, tapping her tooth thoughtfully with the empty knitting needle, "is, what kind of house we should build?"

Dad ran up the stairs and rummaged about in the back of the cupboard on the landing. He came back carrying a rolled-up blueprint.

"I drew up this plan three years ago," he said, as he spread it out on the dining room table.

"Oh, Doggal, I love it," said Mum, dropping her knitting in delight. "It's my dream house."

"I knew you would like it," beamed Dad.

"Yes, and we can build it right next to the bush," said Mum with determination, "nobody can cut down trees on the Reserve."

"That's right," nodded Dad.

"They can't build in our bush either," said Mum smiling.

"That's right, no neighbours." Dad nodded again.

"No windows looking at us."

"Completely hidden," agreed Dad.

"My dream house, hidden in the bush," said Mum sighing with pleasure, "I can't think of anywhere else I'd rather live."

# About the Author

Little House in the Bush is based on Wendy's childhood at Mount Tiger. Later in life, she and her husband Ian, built two cottages on the land so their four children could enjoy a similar childhood. Nowadays, she lives in Australia at the edge of the bush where in addition to possums, there are kangaroos and wombats.

Wendy Hamilton

# Other Children's Books By Wendy Hamilton

## Children's Novels
*Little House in the Cow Paddock*
*The Britwhistles win a Prize*
*The Britwhistles and the Elasticizer*

## Children's Picture books
*The Unlucky Snails*
*The Unlucky Snails go to France*

*These can be found at*
www.zealauspublishing.com

www.ingramcontent.com/pod-product-compliance
Lightning Source LLC
Chambersburg PA
CBHW021151080526
44588CB00008B/292